My Struggle, Your Struggle

Breaking Free From Habitual Sin

David Erik Jones

Dedication

This book is dedicated to Vallarie; my best friend, my lover, my wife. Without your help, support, and forgiveness, I would not be the person I am today. Thank you for all you have done for me and your unconditional love.

Acknowledgements

There is no way I could ever recognize everyone who has influenced me over the years but I do want to say thank you for all they have done to help me. They truly have changed my life. Those changes are now resounding into the lives of others.

So many people have contributed in so many ways to this particular project. In order to show my appreciation I want to acknowledge their contributions publicly.

Vallarie, Stephanie and Kayla thank you for supporting me and loving me through everything. You are the joy of my life and I am so thankful God put us all together. Thank you also for allowing me to open up our history before the world. I pray it is worth it.

To my extended family; thank you. You all have been so supportive over the past few years. The phone calls, the financial support, and the prayers have all been essential. I do not know if I could have endured all of the changes in my life had you not been there for me in so many ways. I know the details of my life that are revealed in this book may make you uncomfortable but I hope I have honored our family and that God will use my story for the good of many.

Tony, I cannot express my gratitude for what you have done for my family. Without your help it would have probably taken years to see this book in print. Thank you brother!

Dane, Tim, David, Kevin, and Dana; your editing, suggestions, words of encouragement, letting me share my vision, and willingness to review my manuscripts have made this a much better book. You were the answers to many prayers as God provided me with friends who have skills which I do not possess. Thank you so much for your time and effort.

Above all, I want to praise my God for all He has done for me. Without Him I would be lost, hopeless and enslaved.

Contents

Forward

Struggles, we all have them; personality quirks, natural tendencies, or the results of circumstances that have shaped us and caused difficulties in life. We do not choose our struggles; they find us or are given to us through various means. Yet we must learn to deal with them and control them so our lives, and the lives of those we love, are not destroyed.

This book was written to share my personal struggle with the overall goal of helping others deal with their own difficulties. I know what it's like to be controlled by sin. I know what it's like to feel hopelessly trapped by a habit you both love and hate. I also know what it's like to overcome a very real and destructive addiction by applying biblical principals to life.

What are my qualifications for writing this book? I am a sinner who has found forgiveness, hope, love, strength, and redemption in Jesus Christ. I am a husband and father who put his family through years of unnecessary pain. I am a minister who almost threw his life away seeking cheap thrills and selfish pleasure. In short, I am human.

As the idea and passion to write my story developed certain goals for this book emerged. First of all, the book had to be honest, direct, and authentic. Secondly, it had to provide real, applicable solutions based upon the Bible and my own real life experiences. Third, it had to be easy to read with short chapters. Fourth, it had to contain scriptural references to allow for more in depth study for those who might want to go deeper on their own. I hope these goals are adequately accomplished.

However, I feel I must warn you this book is not for everyone. It contains some very frank, personal information about my addiction to pornography. The account of my struggle is not graphic, but is honest. I sincerely hope those who read this book will be able to sense the battle that raged within me as I tried to break free and at the same time give them the courage and weapons necessary to overcome their own struggles.

Also, I wrote this book not only as a man who has had to deal with a sinful habit but as a Christian and pastor as well. I openly admit I am trying to share my faith and offer hope to those who are trapped in a sinful lifestyle or dealing with other deep seeded problems. This does not mean the book is only useful to someone currently caught in sin but it should be helpful for everyone who reads it. After all, everyone has to deal with temptations and sinful tendencies. No one is immune; we all have struggles.

"For I know that nothing good dwells in me, that is, in my flesh; for the willing is present in me, but the doing of the good is not. For the good that I want, I do not do, but I practice the very evil that I do not want. But if I am doing the very thing I do not want, I am no longer the one doing it, but sin which dwells in me." (Romans 7:18-20)

My Struggle

W e were in a garage. I don't remember a lot of other details about that day, except for the magazine. It reminded me of a *Sears* catalog. It was heavy, thick, and had full-color, glossy pages. It was the first *Playboy* I had ever seen. I was in the second grade.

My friend had found the magazine. I guess it was his dad's. We snuck it into the garage to check it out. Two little kids flipping through the pages, making wise cracks and laughing. The whole time I knew we shouldn't be looking. I knew we were doing something that eight-year-old boys were not supposed to do, but I liked it; it was thrilling. Little did I know this would be the beginning of a life long struggle with pornography.

Yet this was not my first encounter with sex. My battle with sexual addiction started at an early age, so young that I cannot remember the first time I had a sexual thought. My earliest recollections of sexual experiences go back to the age of about five. That may sound exaggerated but I promise you it is not. In the next few chapters I will share some of the events that shaped me as a little boy. I will not go into vivid detail about these encounters but I can assure you with all of my heart I was not only aware of sexuality at such a young age, but I acted upon sexual urges as well.

The purpose of this book is not to delve into the mind of a child nor is it to seek out scientific data about children and sexual experiences. However, I do want to share my story in hopes of helping others find a way to overcome habitual sin. Some of the information you will read is very personal and may embarrass you. I know a few people will be revolted and others will think my experiences are rather mild compared to their own. My intention is not to shock people but instead to offer hope. I have to be honest and open to help you see within the depths of my soul so you can understand the extent of my struggle.

The events of my childhood set the stage for what was to come later in my life. I can still remember the thrill, the excitement, and the secrecy that surrounded a young boy's "dirty" thoughts and acts. Was I just curious? Perhaps, but I still knew there was something "naughty" about it all. I knew some of the things I began to do were not to be done openly and were supposed to be "secret." This only seemed to increase the thrill and excitement.

There were other factors that influenced me too. I grew up in the seventies and eighties and the sexual revolution was in full swing. I can only now, as a middle-aged man, look back and see what kind of affect the sexually saturated culture has had on me, the people I love, and my life in general. I praise God I am not in prison, dead from AIDS, or suffering from the results of a painful divorce. I praise my Savior, Jesus Christ, for paying the price for my sins and redeeming my life and giving me hope. It is only by the grace of God that I am alive and able to share my story. This is my struggle.

The Beginning

From an early age I was interested in sex. Even before that fateful day in the garage I had been curious about sex. It is impossible for me to pinpoint the first time I acted upon a sexual impulse but I do know it was before the age of eight. We lived in a small Texas town in the early Seventies when I was between the ages of three and seven. I can vividly remember several sexual events that occurred there. They have been stamped on my mind. There were at least a few other sexual experiences in my young life but they have become foggy with time and I don't want to speculate about that which is unclear.

I want to reiterate that I am not trying to shock anyone or to embellish these events in any way. However, I do hope people will see even young children are greatly affected by sexual imagery and stimulation. What we see, what we are exposed to, and what we hear impacts our views of life and greatly influences the choices we make and who we eventually become. You don't have to be a teenager or young adult to be negatively influenced by images and words.

I am not sure why I was so interested in sex when I was so young, but I do remember overhearing someone (perhaps my older brothers) making comments about sex, and I wanted to discover more. I was young but very intrigued. My interest was peaked and I acted upon the little information I had.

When I was just five or six years old I tried to carry out a sexual act with a younger girl. Although I had no idea what it really meant, I attempted to do to her exactly what I had heard described. I wasn't old enough to fully understand sex, but I was old enough to be curious. I still remember that day very clearly. It has haunted me for years.

Many children "play house" and act as "mommy and daddy." This is nothing new and would probably be considered normal. Yet it just reveals how greatly children are influenced by the world around them. I have talked to other people and have found these kinds of actions are not rare. Kids copy what they see and hear. This is a reality.

Another incident in my childhood occurred behind the small school in town, on a sand dune. I don't really know what prompted my actions but I basically dropped my pants and fondled myself. There I was, on the backside of the hill, half naked in the sand, a little boy acting upon an impulse he didn't understand, dealing with ideas and emotions far beyond his comprehension. My age of innocence didn't last long.

I remember those events and more. Writing this book has caused me to search my heart and memory some thirty years later. At times I've been overcome with shame even though I know a five year old is unable to make major moral choices. I kept all of this inside, bottled up as personal secrets for so long. Only recently have I shared these events with my wife for the first time. Even then, I was still somewhat embarrassed to tell her about them. Yet being able to talk about it, cry about it, and deal with it has been good for me. It has been a painful but liberating experience.

Some people might say these kinds of activities are normal and a natural part of growing up. They might reason it is healthy for a child to explore his sexuality and become familiar with his body. Yet it was just a foreshadowing of the events that would shape my life in such a dramatic way.

Even after all the soul searching I have not been able to determine why I was drawn to sex so early in my life. To the best of my knowledge I was never molested or harmed sexually in any way. There are some very faint recollections of an older boy (a high school aged neighbor) who may have encouraged me to do some things, but I am not sure. I don't want to draw attention to this because I cannot say for certain it is absolutely true. Yet there are lingering images in my mind of events that perhaps shaped me at this point in my life. The recollections are not clear and I rarely think about these phantom memories. However, this could explain why I acted out sexually when I was so young. Once again I am not trying to blame anyone or even speculate as to what might have happened. But it does seem relevant. It could have a lot to do with my premature interest in sex.

I've tried to look at other possibilities as well. Back in the early seventies we didn't have graphic video games and reality television. *Captain Kangaroo* was my favorite television show and I loved Glen Campbell's *Rhinestone Cowboy*. They were in no way raunchy or filled with sexual innuendos. Also, my parents were careful about what we watched and listened to in those years. I was not exposed to sex at home other than listening to my older brothers and their friends (who were themselves still in elementary school at the time). To the best of my recollection there were no other influences that would have stirred my interest when I was so young. I have searched my mind and cannot pinpoint any certain event or moment that might explain my curiosity. All I can say with certainty is that I was interested and had begun to act upon my thoughts.

Although I don't know what initially caused me to want to explore sex, I do know that my first view of pornography had a dramatic impact in my life. Porn gripped me and nearly destroyed me. My addiction to pornography started when I was just a kid, but it has been the most difficult battle of my life. It greatly affected who I would become and it led me down a path of darkness.

The Pictures Never Fade

That day in the garage changed my life. It was the first time I looked at pornography but definitely would not be my last. It was about a year later when I looked at another magazine. Some older boys had a *Playboy* magazine in a wooded area. I literally can still see one of those images in my mind. I was in third grade.

I not only remember the picture but recall taking it a step further. I actually mimicked the scene in the shower when I had a friend stay over one night. We were just joking around and didn't have any type of sexual encounter. I told him about the image I had seen and then I acted it out. As I did, I pulled the shower curtain down accidentally. It made quite a commotion and my mother came in and asked if we were okay. I lied and made up some excuse as to why the shower curtain had fallen. I dodged a bullet, but this was only the beginning of the many lies I would tell. Lies told to people I loved. Lies I told myself.

I was only nine years old but had begun to act upon the images. I was enthralled with nudity and sex. I was eager to learn more and there was plenty to capture my attention. At that age I had little self-control or real ability to discern the depths of sin I was being drawn into. All I knew was the thrill and pleasure and allure of the magazines. I wanted more and never even thought about the long-term effects. No one warned me about these things. No one even suspected I was beginning to form such a destructive habit. Looking back, I can see how these few encounters drew me in and set me upon a path of destruction. How I wish I had been caught! How I wish I had never taken those first steps! How I wish my experience with pornography had ended there!

There is another memory that is clear in my mind. Later that year I overheard a conversation one of my brothers had with a friend. They were talking about things I had never heard before. I don't think they knew I was listening. The conversation was between them, I was eavesdropping.

It was after this conversation I began to more aggressively explore my sexuality. This really opened up a new avenue of curiosity. Sex had taken on a new level of feeling and excitement. It had gone from the pages and images to experiencing my own pleasure. I would never be the same.

It was about this time I also began to notice sexual lyrics in songs. Music soon became a very real and powerful source of sexual thought and excitement in my life. Music is a powerful conduit for ideas and imagery, and it can have an amazing effect in a person's life: positive or negative. Later in life music became a wonderful gift from God, but as a young boy and teenager, it only pulled me further into the darkness.

The music-video revolution was a big factor in my teenage years. *MTV* was new and the videos were able to bring to life the sexual songs I had grown to love. I now had images of women in revealing clothing and sexual situations to go along with the provocative words I had memorized. Once the scenes were in my head, it was easy to recall them every time I heard the music or sang the song to myself. (In fact, I can still vividly recall some of the videos I have not seen in over twenty years. The combination of music and imagery is powerful.) The older I got the more I could fantasize to my favorite songs. Country, pop, or rap, it really didn't matter, they were all full of references to sex and I was quick to pick up on the messages.

I don't want to give you the idea sex was all I thought about and everyday I was caught up in sexual activity. I would go days, weeks, or even months without any specific event. Yet something would happen. A song, a picture, or something else would prompt another onslaught. Each time the attraction and risk would increase. Each time I was drawn a little deeper into the darkness. I was slowly being sucked into a habit that would eventually nearly consume me. It happened slowly at first but then began to accelerate.

Puberty

I cannot remember a time in my life when I was unaware of sex. However, puberty ushered in more urgency and risk taking. As my body matured and the excitement increased so did my desire for more sexual fulfillment. I was willing to do just about anything to find sexual pleasure. It was truly a driving force and would shape the person I would become.

I cannot fully express the impact of pornography at this point in my life. A man in our neighborhood had a vast assortment of magazines stacked in his bedroom closet. Some of the local kids knew about it and we would sometimes go over to his house, while the adults were gone, and go through the pictures with his kids. I was introduced to new images. The magazines were no longer just about nude women in sexy poses. The content became far more intense and sexual. It was my first taste of hardcore porn.

I became completely captivated and addicted to pornography at this point in my life. It had a power over me that was beyond expression. Unless you have been held captive by an addiction you may not understand how this affected my life. I was willing to do anything I could to find pornography. Once when this family was out of town on vacation, I literally broke into their house to steal some of the magazines. I still remember the pounding of my heart, the sick feeling in my gut, and the pressing fear I would be caught. The closet was empty, so I rummaged through their home. I looked in every drawer and shelf, under the bed, and in every possible hiding place. I found nothing and snuck back out. I felt dirty. I was so ashamed of myself.

After the family returned they began to ask questions. It was obvious someone had been in their house. I heard my Mom talking to the wife of the man who had the porn. She suspected a neighborhood kid had been involved, but they couldn't prove who it was. Mom, of course, never knew I was the culprit, but I knew who was guilty. I knew what I had done.

I am so overwhelmed with remorse when I think about it now, but at the time I was so driven I was willing to risk everything to just have a look. I had a problem. I was addicted. By this time I knew it was morally wrong. I knew it was sinful. I knew I was living in shame and guilt, but I was hooked. The allure was too strong and I wanted more, no matter the consequences. The fear of being caught and the knowledge that I was sinning was not enough to stop me. A hunger burned within me.

I have watched documentaries about people who are addicted to crack or other drugs. These people are willing to steal, lie, and even murder in order to get their next fix. They will sell their bodies for drugs, turn away from loved ones, and destroy their health for just a moment of pleasure. I truly can sympathize and have a deep compassion for them. I know what it is like to be driven by a habit. I know what it is like to do ungodly things just to feel the rush. You may not understand how a person can become addicted to pornography. I really don't expect everyone to know what its like, but with all of my heart I can testify it is a reality. Once the poison is in your veins you want more. The excitement is real. The desire lingers. The temptation to look just one more time constantly whispers your name.

No one knew where I was headed. No one knew what was going on inside of me. My view of women and sex were being distorted as seeds of lust were being planted in my soul.

A couple of my friends and I would find porn from time to time. People would discard magazines carelessly or we would find a copy at the dump ground. Some kids would even steal their dad's porn. We collected a small "stash" and hid it behind the fence in the alley for a while. I could hardly wait to grab the "dirty books" and go to our makeshift tree house for a few minutes of excitement. I really didn't like looking at the magazines with other boys; it made it a little strange. Becoming aroused by the images embarrassed me. I didn't want the guys to know. I preferred to be alone in a secluded place.

Sometimes I would sneak a few pages of pornography into my house. I found places to hide the snippets; my favorite place was under the bathroom sink.

I worked loose the small piece of wood at the bottom of the vanity so I could slip in my favorite pictures. The wooden piece would fit right back into place, as if it had never been touched. Once the pictures were safely hidden, I would wait until late at night or until I was alone to indulge. However, I wouldn't leave the photos in the house long because I was afraid someone in my family would find them. I constantly checked to make sure my hiding place was undisturbed. I was somewhat paranoid, always wondering when my secret would be revealed. After a week or so the fear of being caught would take over and I would throw the pictures away. The thought of being found out was terrible, but not enough to keep me from doing it all over again. The fear would subside, and I would repeat the process time after time.

Eventually I collected my own private stash and hid it in an old abandoned cellar behind our church. I would sneak off by myself and slip into the cellar to gaze lustfully at the images in the dim, musty, cement cavity. My lust had driven me into a "dungeon."

This was directly behind the church in which I was later baptized and married. It was the church that opened my eyes to the word of God. It was the place that would help me begin my long struggle to overcome pornography. It was the church where I first felt called to ministry. It is an ironic contrast that describes my life.

Acts of Shame

I didn't want everyone to know who I was. I was supposed to have it all together. You see, I was one of the local good kids. I was a straight-A student, an athlete, a church boy, and an all around nice guy. I was literally the homecoming king and valedictorian. I was the kind of guy that no one every suspects is caught up in pornography.

Despite my addiction, I was tender hearted and really did care about people. I lived two lives. I knew how to act in public and how to treat girls most of the time. I truly wanted to be a good kid and never wanted anyone to know the dark secrets that lingered in my soul. I sincerely wanted to be good. I wanted to be kind. I wanted to be the young man that a father would be proud to let his daughter date. That was who I wanted to be. Yet I knew there was darkness within me.

Yes, I know every teenage boy has a strong sex drive. But I was in hyper drive! The pornography was feeding my sexual desires and causing them to work overtime. At the same time, pornography was warping my view of sex. It was unhealthy and dangerous. I had a problem and it was growing worse.

The teenage years opened up new temptations when I began to date. As I grew so did my intense desire for sexual pleasure, but I didn't act out upon these desires with every girl I dated. Sure we kissed and began to explore our sexuality, but I was seldom really aggressive or unkind. I wanted them to like me. I respected them, and I didn't want to ruin our relationship. These were sincere feelings and a part of who I was. I did want to be a gentleman! I really wanted to do what was right!

But there were also girls I thought were "experienced," and I guess, looking back, I had no respect for them. (This was an error on my part. They didn't deserve this; I was wrong.) So I would openly and aggressively try to have sex with them. On several occasions I said and did things that shocked me.

On one occasion after my freshman year in school, I invited a girl over to my house. I was the only one at home and her family was about to move out of town. I had heard rumors that she was experienced, so I thought I would give it a shot. We were not dating; I just called her up out of the blue. She had no idea what I was up to and was completely surprised when I asked her very directly to have sex with me. She was taken aback, and I was overcome with shame. The darkness had broken through. She saw the beast that raged within me.

The drive to have sex was strong, and I kept feeding my urges with images and fantasies. Instead of running from the pornography, I let it shape me and my ideals of sex. The more I indulged and exposed my mind to the images the more I wanted to experience. Pornography didn't help me control my urges. In fact, pornography made them stronger. It increased my desire for sex greatly. This completely defies the notion that if you indulge a little it will help you remain in control. The truth is if you feed a desire it will only grow stronger and demand more attention.

I praise God now I didn't have sex that day. I am so grateful she walked away. I am so thankful that wasn't my first time and it didn't happen that way. But I could see even then I was acting out, aggressively and harmfully. Under the right circumstances I could be a very mean and dangerous person. It scared me. I saw a monster within that seemed to take control occasionally. The darkness would rise up and take over. The urges demanded more attention. I felt like Jekyll and Hyde.

The teenage girls I treated so harshly were often surprised too because they could see a monster, someone they didn't expect to see, someone they didn't know was there. I could see they lost all respect for me. I knew they would never feel comfortable around me again. It was a terrible feeling, so I desperately fought to keep everything a secret. It horrified me to think my parents or my teachers would find out who I "really" was.

I haven't forgotten these girls. I have often wanted to apologize for my behavior. Perhaps someday I will have the chance. (Maybe I am in some way trying to apologize by sharing these experiences in this book.)

I hope I didn't leave scars in their lives. I pray I didn't cause them great emotional pain.

This is just one of the long-lasting effects that remains in my own heart and perhaps in theirs as well. The weight of it all has rested on my soul. As a parent of two teenage daughters today, it makes me sick to think of the way I treated some of the girls in my past. I would never want anybody to treat my daughters that way. The girls I dated didn't deserve to be so disrespected. They didn't deserve to be groped and pressured. They were not at fault; I was. I chose to treat them poorly. I chose to act out on my own sexual urges. I am the only one to blame.

As I got older and began to date regularly, I became more aggressive, even towards the girls I respected and wanted to treat well. The more I experienced, the more I wanted to experience. Hugging and kissing were no longer enough. I began to treat every girl I dated as a sex object. I could see myself becoming more and more assertive but I didn't want to stop. I cared for my girl friends, but I seldom consider how my actions were affecting them. I was driven by an overwhelming desire to fulfill my craving for sexual fulfillment. Their feelings, their well-being, and their futures really didn't matter to me at the time. The tender, compassionate young man was fading and a beast was taking his place. I hated myself.

There were a couple of times when I almost had sex. Although I looked forward to the first time, I was afraid. What would it be like? Was I "man" enough? Would I make a fool of myself? These fears actually held me back on a few occasions when the opportunity arose. On other occasions, the girl I was with chose to hold off. I am so grateful now they made the right choice because at the time I was more than willing to go all the way. I praise God for that today and see He was protecting me even when I didn't know it. His grace was covering me long before I ever even knew His grace existed.

As my physical experiences increased with my girlfriends so did my thirst for pornography. I can see now it was the pornography, sexually explicit music, movies, and TV that increased my desire to have sex. Everywhere I went there it was, constantly begging for my attention. I have heard it is normal for a young man to have sexual urges and that pornography is just one way to "healthfully" explore sex and to release pent up urges. This is a lie. Pornography only multiplies the urge for sexual activity. Even more disturbing is the fact pornography promotes various forms of risky sex and increases the likelihood of rape, incest, and deviant sexual activity. Pornography is in no way "healthy."

Pornography not only increased my desire to have sex but also created another problem. As a teenager I seemed almost unable to control the urge to masturbate. I would sneak out of the house sometimes at one, two or even three in the morning and masturbate outside. This doesn't include the times I would do so in the bathroom or elsewhere. It truly became a real addiction. I was obsessed. Many people probably don't think this is abnormal. I know statistically most teenage boys do masturbate. However, I was over-the-edge. I will not go into any further detail here, but I can assure you, I was acting in ways that were not right or normal. Again, I believe the pornography only increased the desire and fed my habit.

To make matters worse, about the time I was a junior in high school my oldest brother bought my parents a satellite dish, you know the ones that were about ten foot wide and took up a whole corner of the backyard. It was great to have so many new channels, but it also brought in new temptations.

We didn't have a subscription to the *Playboy Channel* or any other adult network but they would have "sneak previews." When I was home alone or late at night, I would turn the satellite over to the adult stations. There was enough material to keep me captivated. As I think about this, I am amazed no one ever caught me. I have often wondered if my parents knew what I was doing. I have wondered if anyone noticed the TV on in the living room at 3 AM. If they did, no one ever confronted me or asked me about it.

I will not go into more vivid specifics, but I must say I took amazing risks and would literally lay awake at night just waiting for an opportunity to find some time to indulge my urges. I look back now and wonder how I could have been so caught up with it all, but realize too, I truly had a problem. Though I feared being caught back then, I can now see it would have been a blessing. If my secret life had been revealed perhaps I could have received the help I needed before my struggle consumed me. But I was too afraid to reach out. I thought I was abnormal. I wanted to talk about it with someone but whom could I turn to? Who would understand? Who would accept me? I felt like a pervert. Maybe I was.

As I wrote earlier, movies, TV, videos, songs, and the sexual culture I grew up in made my battle worse. No matter where I went, what I watched, or what I listened to, I was saturated with sexual imagery. It was a constant onslaught of stimulation. It drew me deeper and deeper into sexual addiction. Even though I had come to understand the fact I was sinning against God and acting in shameful ways, I could not stop. The allure was too great. The excitement was too much. I was addicted.

I will not relate all I did. There is no reason to go into more detail. I have tried to share with you enough information to help you see the depth of my struggle. I have tried to show you the power pornography has had in my life. My intention was not to be too graphic or improper, however, I wanted you to see how real and overwhelming my problem was. I was truly enslaved.

Hope?

At the age of sixteen I accepted Jesus Christ as my Lord and Savior. The more I attended church, the more I struggled with sin and shame and forgiveness. I believed the words of the Bible and I had godly people in my life who taught me about Jesus. I wanted my sins to be washed away. I wanted to go to heaven. So one spring afternoon I went to my pastor's house, knocked on the door and told him I wanted to accept Jesus Christ as my Lord and Savior. That day I asked Jesus to forgive me and cleanse me of my sins. He did.

I have heard people share their testimonies and tell about how God took away their desire to drink or gamble. This was not the case for me. I wish I could say I was set free and never acted impure again, but I did. The temptations didn't go away even though I knew I was living in sin. I would resist for weeks and even months at a time, until I would give in to my sexual urges. After that, I would slip into guilt and shame and despair, which would lead to careless acts of sexual fulfillment. It was a vicious cycle that never ended. I really began to believe there was no hope for me. I honestly could not imagine life without pornography.

Since I could not control my habit I thought perhaps I hadn't been saved. Maybe I didn't believe the truth. Perhaps I hadn't done it right. Or maybe it was all "bull" anyway. At the time I thought becoming a Christian was supposed to make me feel better not worse!

The guilt, shame, confusion, and inner struggle only intensified as I grew up. I knew I was sinning. I knew I was caught in sexual perversion. I knew I needed to change, but I couldn't. My desires and sexual explorations only increased. I thought I might grow out of my struggle, but it only became worse. Praying didn't seem to help, and trying harder to be good never had a long-term affect. Even reading the Bible religiously never made me stop for long. What was I missing? Why couldn't I control myself? Why wouldn't God make it go away?

As I dealt with these questions, I would often sit in church and feel terrible. If I were in the middle of a binge, I would feel shame and guilt and would cry out to Jesus for forgiveness, and the strength to stop. If I were living in a brief time of abstinence, I would sit and watch the preacher and hope God didn't want me to preach someday, even though I knew I would. But how could I preach? I was so full of shame and impurity. Could someone like me ever be a minister?

I felt so alone, so perverted, so torn inside. I never talked to my friends, brothers, or anyone else about my struggle, so I never knew if I was way over-the-top. I would often reason that I was normal and that all boys did these things. A few of the magazines I would read would suggest that all young men masturbated, and it was good and normal. Of course this information brought me comfort. It was good enough for me and gave me an excuse to continue. After all, the "experts" seemed to think it was "normal and helpful." (I loved it when someone or something justified my sin.)

Sex was portrayed everywhere, yet was still "taboo" in church and, for the most part, at home too. I was never really ever taught specifically about these things, so I made my own discoveries and choices. I liked the images. I liked masturbating. I liked the thrill of making out and trying to go as far as I could with girls. It was exciting. Yet I was aware by this time of the truth; I was headed in the wrong direction.

As I mentioned earlier, I did want to talk to someone about my struggle. I just didn't know whom I could trust. I didn't want to embarrass myself, or them. I thought about talking to my Dad on several occasions but never could muster up the courage. I didn't want him to think less of me. I knew my Mom would talk to me, but I was just too embarrassed. I wish now I had reached out for help. But at the time I just couldn't bring myself to ask the questions I needed to. I couldn't tell others who I really was and what I had been doing, so I kept my secret. I felt trapped and alone. I felt imprisoned.

I don't want to give anyone the impression my parents didn't care. I know they did and still do.

Mom has always been very straightforward about life, and I trust her and Dad greatly. Yet there was just something within me that didn't want to talk to them about sex. I guess this is natural. It just seems so much easier to talk to someone other than your parents about these things. Yet parents are such an important link. I regret not going to them. I believe they would have helped me had I asked. They were there. I just never took that first step towards freedom by asking for their help.

Today, I pray my daughters know they can come to my wife and me anytime and speak openly with us, whatever their problems or questions may be. I hope they will take advantage of the love and understanding we can offer them. I pray they don't make the same mistake I made.

Had I talked to my Mom and Dad, I probably could have been set free. I know they would have helped me and changed the course of my life. But instead of asking questions, I hid it all in the shadows, hoping no one would find out. I let the darkness hold me back because I was afraid of letting others know who I really was inside. Instead of reaching out to those who loved me the most, I drew back into the lonely prison of addiction.

I thought I hid it all well. I know some family members had to know more than I thought they did at the time. Seven of us lived in a small three bedroom house, so there wasn't a whole lot of privacy. Also, I didn't always act correctly around my sisters. I know my actions may have had an effect on them. This is one of the greatest sorrows of my life. I never harmed them physically, but I said and did things I shouldn't have, when they were around. I know I am forgiven, but I am haunted by my actions and the potential effects I may have had in their lives. I set a poor example for my little sisters. That still troubles me. They may not remember, but I do, it has haunted me for so long. I am so sorry.

Was there any hope? Did being a Christian make any difference? Once I received Jesus as my Lord and Savior, a battle began to rage within me: sexual desire versus a pulling towards God. I wish I could say I responded to God, and that I was noble and righteous and quickly surrendered to purity. I didn't. I guess I always thought it would all just go away. I guess I really believed I would simply "grow out of it." I thought I would never have to worry about it all once I was married. Isn't that the way it happens on TV? You play around, do what feels good, and then settle into a marriage. The boyhood fantasies and pornography were just supposed to go away.

Unfortunately, the pictures never fade and the ideals of sex that are formed by pornography linger. You can't simply leave the images in your childhood. You don't suddenly forget what you have seen and the desires that were generated. Pornography literally twists the amazing gift of sex and turns it into a selfish, sinful, and dirty act. God has blessed us with our sexuality. Pornography degrades it. The images never fade.

Marriage

Near the end of my junior year in high school I began to see I was in trouble. One of my brothers was in college at the time, and I was planning to move in with him after I graduated. I could just imagine the party life. I was excited about the sexual atmosphere at college, and would often fantasize about the sexual explorations ahead. After all that was all I knew about the college life. That was what the movies and music videos showed me. That is what I thought it was all about; parities, beer, women, and plenty of sex.

Yet at the same time something within me was shouting a warning. Something within me was well aware of the darkness that lingered in my heart. There was a war raging within. I understand now it was God working in my life. I can see it was God intervening and drawing me to Him. At the time though, I just knew I had a foreboding within me that feared what was ahead. I couldn't put my finger on it, but had an underlying feeling I was headed for public shame, great harm, and perhaps even death, if I continued on my destructive sexual path. I couldn't fight the deep-seeded emotion and dread. Something needed to happen. Something had to change.

Late in my junior year I began to pray for a wife. I thought I knew the girl I wanted to spend the rest of my life with, and asked God for the chance to marry her. I prayed that if she wasn't the one, that He would send someone else. I would lie in bed and struggle with the inner conflict and ask God to send me the person I needed to marry. He sent Vallarie. We fell in love and soon began to talk about marriage even though we were both still just seventeen.

I cannot say we were sexually pure. I cannot say we immediately gave ourselves wholly to God. I wish I could. I wish my struggle had ended. I wish I never had to fight a sexual urge again, but this was not the case. My struggle remained.

Yet for the first time, even before we were married, I was finally able to talk to someone openly about sex. For the first time in my life I was able to share my struggle with another person. I had found more than a lover. I had found a friend in whom I could confide. I cannot remember ever having a real, open, and honest talk about sex with anyone until I met Val. Yes, my mother was very good to give us some details and advice and so on, but I was never completely honest with her. Yes, we did have some sex education in school but it had nothing to do with reality, it was a text book! We even had at least one lesson at a church youth meeting about sex, but it was vague and ineffective. I needed more. I needed someone to really talk to. I didn't have a man in whom I felt comfortable with, someone to go to for advice. I didn't have a way to express my concern and struggle, so I held it all in and let the lust shape my life.

My father loves me and has been a great dad. I love him and respect him more than any other man I know, but we didn't have an open, close relationship at that time. He set many good examples for me and taught me great things, but I didn't feel comfortable talking to him about sex. Perhaps that was just my feeling of shame. Maybe I just never asked. Maybe I was too embarrassed. I don't fault my Dad at all. I do wish we had talked about sex. I do wish I could have asked about masturbation and virginity and those kinds of things. I wanted someone to tell me I wasn't a pervert. I wanted someone to help me, but I just did not know where to turn.

I wanted someone to talk to, but I never felt "safe" enough to share my secrets until I met Vallarie. She was the first person I was able to talk with about my darkness. She listened and didn't judge me. We both shared our experiences, fears, hurts, and the pain we each felt. We both really wanted to obey God and to live in purity, but we just didn't know how. Unfortunately we didn't abstain, although we talked about it, prayed about it, and committed time and again to wait until we were married. We both greatly regret this and wish deeply we had waited. The Lord has forgiven us, but the facts remain and we both are remorseful over the choices we made. It took us years to deal with some of the issues that came from our bad decisions. We had to learn to trust one another, let go of the past, and to talk honestly about our feelings.

The scars of sexual sin do not fade over night. Hollywood and pornography don't show that side of immorality. They don't reveal the truth. They only show the instant gratification and selfish pleasure. They ignore the consequences and sell a false reality, an imitation of the real thing, a counterfeit of sex that never lives up to the image.

The consequences are real. In reality, the pain, guilt, and effects last much longer than the moment of excitement and pleasure. It's simply not worth it. I wish I had realized that then.

At the time, Val and I both needed someone and God put us together. Three months after our high school graduation we married in that small church. We were immature and heaven only knows how we were able to survive those first few years of marriage, but we did. We thought we had it all figured out and enjoyed a passionate sex life. I thought my struggles where gone forever. I was wrong.

Addicted

T hough mine and Val's sex life was good, I was plagued by the images and ideas that had been driven into my head. Sex wasn't completely fulfilling because it never met the expectation I had created in my mind. Years of Hollywood images and pornographic influence had twisted my view of sex. I had false expectations about sex and marriage and reality could never match the fantasy world. This left a void, a longing, and a dangerous thirst within.

The truth is pornography and Hollywood sell false versions of sex. They give us an incorrect view of something God gave us to enjoy and build closer marriages. However, the images had implanted in my mind a fantasy world that didn't exist. I judged our sex life based on the twisted fantasies. My warped view made me think something was missing. Instead of enjoying the great gift God had given us, I wanted to make it better. I wanted it to be just like I had seen it portrayed for so many years. When it wasn't, I began to think something was wrong with me. I thought maybe I was inadequate.

I also put a lot of pressure on Val. Instead of feeling loved and appreciated, she began to fill used and worthless. My distorted view of intimacy was causing more pain than closeness, more harm than good.

It took me years to figure this out, but it was and still is a constant influence. The images don't fade. The expectations are there though unrealistic. This led to a constant desire for more pleasurable sex, and Val could never meet my expectations. It was not her fault, but was simply the result of all the sexual images and lies I had been exposed to throughout my life.

You can probably see how pornography and the false realities have greatly impacted our marriage. In fact, they nearly destroyed our marriage.

Shamefully, I would try to introduce her into the world of porn. I thought it would "spice up" our love life. I thought it would turn her on and open up a whole new world of pleasure for both of us. (That is a lie. I was only truly seeking my own fulfillment but justified the lie by saying it would bring us both more pleasure.) Repeatedly I tried to draw her down into the dark world of sexual smut but she refused. I praise God for her character and morality and willingness to resist my pressure. By God's grace I am blessed with a wonderful and compassionate and strong wife. She stood her ground and helped me to face the darkness within.

Today we are healing and we are learning to enjoy the gift God has given us. It has taken some time, some very frank discussions, and years of dealing with the problem, but we are finding freedom as a married couple. Thank you, Val. Thank you, God.

It has not been easy. There have been many challenges along the way, some in unseen surprises. Vallarie and I were blessed early with two amazing daughters. We will be forever grateful for these two wonderful blessings from God. They are tremendous sources of joy in our lives. But with children come changes. Attentions shift and privacy dissipates. Yet my sexual desires didn't diminish. Slowly I was pulled back into my own private world of sexual experience. Marriage had not solved my underlying sexual addiction. It remained there, below the surface, waiting to pull me back under.

To make matters worse, Val was dealing with jealousy issues. She knew I had struggled in the past with pornography and felt she wasn't attractive enough for me, especially after giving birth. She always compared herself to the images in the magazines. This fed her fear that I would leave her for someone more attractive. As time passed that fear increased, and I withdrew.

Val could never understand I found her very attractive, even after childbirth. I tried to explain to her my problem with pornography had nothing to do with her appearance, but had everything to do with my sexual addiction. I wasn't disappointed in her looks at all. (In fact I still see her as one of the most attractive women I have ever known.) I was just drawn to the thrill porn produced. She was never the problem; I was. My sinful habit would have continued no matter what she looked like and no matter whom

I had married. There were great underlying issues that needed to be resolved in my life. I was addicted and I had to deal with that before our marriage could grow.

When our oldest daughter was born we were still very young and had been married just over a year. At that time we hadn't developed the deep communication skills we have today. As a result I began to pull back and withhold information. Instead of telling her how I felt and sharing my struggles with her, I would hide it all and lie to cover it up. She was not at fault. Certainly we both needed to learn to talk openly and freely about everything once again, but I chose to lie and hide my addiction. I damaged our marriage. I broke her trust and respect. I nearly destroyed everything we had dreamed about, all the plans we had made. I nearly ended our marriage because I would not let go of pornography.

As time passed I slowly picked up where I had left off. It is kind of funny; I was always too embarrassed to buy porn, but I never had to because you can find pornography if you look hard enough. I found magazines on the side of the road. I would pick out the "spicy" rated "R" movies and I would even read Val's old romance novels. (Yes romance novels! They are very graphic and can really fire up your imagination.) There was always a way to find a cheap thrill.

The "old me" had returned. They old cycle was back. I would go without for a month or two and then begin to thirst for more. I would find a fix. I would indulge the darkness and then hate myself for weeks.

The whole time I was hiding everything from Val. If she asked me about porn, I would lie and get angry with her. I would accuse her of not trusting me and make her feel bad. But every year or two I would break down and confess my sins only to return to the old habits. I don't know how she put up with it. I don't know how we made it through. Those were difficult years.

Then things got worse. Around 1998 I was introduced to internet pornography. A man in the same office building I worked in was on-line. I had heard of the quick and easy access to porn via the internet but really doubted it. Yet the curiosity built. It was enough temptation to give it a shot even though this meant using his computer in his office, since I was not connected to the internet.

One day in his office while doing legitimate research, I sheepishly typed "sex" into the search engine. A whole new provocative world was opened up to me. I was shocked at the ease and degree of pornography online. It was so simple, quick, and thrilling. It was the beginning of another battle in my war against sexual addiction. Until then I would just stumble across pornography, but now I could easily access it.

I would find excuses to use his computer while he was out of the office. I could always come up with a reason to do more "research." To this day I am not sure if he ever knew what I was up to. Perhaps one day I will look him up and ask him to forgive me. He is one more example of the people I used and hurt.

I fully realized there was a great risk involved in using his computer and internet connection. I tried to hide my tracks but really had very little skill. I feared I would get caught and lose my job. Yet I couldn't stop. Not long after that first internet experience, I talked Val into getting a computer and going on-line at the house. She was leery but really had no idea as to the depth of my problem. I would lie to her and tell her I never looked at anything like that. I hated lying to her, but not enough to stop and tell her the truth.

Over the next few years I began to delve deeper and deeper into internet pornography. I would never pay for images because I didn't want to leave a trail that would lead back to my habit. There were always enough free sites and images, so I never had to worry about paying. It was so easy.

Yet I was paying dearly. I was paying from my soul. I was paying by going down a road of destruction. I was putting my entire life on the line: my wife, my kids, my job, my calling. But the guilt, the shame, and the risk of losing it all was not enough to make me stop. I was sinking and really never believed I would ever change.

I knew it was wrong. I knew the danger, and I knew it wasn't worth it, but I couldn't seem to stop. No matter how many times I prayed. No matter how badly I hated myself. No matter how often I told myself it was wrong, I just kept going. I was truly addicted. I had a real problem and it was getting worse.

You may not understand how someone can be drawn into something as ugly and harmful as pornography. You may not know what its like to desire ungodly things even though you despise what they mean and how they affect others. You may have never been pulled by a dark force into a habit that grows like a cancer in your soul, but I do, and there are millions like me. I know there are millions of people in the United States alone who are drawn into brothels and adult video stores every day. There are men and women who can't seem to stop going back to that forbidden website over and over again. Sexual addictions are real, powerful, and destructive. Statistics clearly show we have a problem of epidemic proportions here in America. Pornography and sexual addiction has in some way affected every one of us, either directly or indirectly.

I have watched television programs in which men are busted after soliciting sex on-line. In an instant their lives are changed forever. Most people probably see them as monsters, and perhaps in a sense they are, but I understand their side of the story too. I am in no way trying to justify what they have done, nor am I saying they should not be prosecuted and punished. Yet I would be willing to say the vast majority of these men have a pornography problem. It probably began when they were young, and has gone unchecked for years. Porn was probably the seed that grew into an unhealthy and harmful desire that led them to act so dangerously. This is not an excuse but rather an explanation.

We've also all seen exposés and news reports centered on politicians, teachers, businessmen, or preachers who have been caught in improprieties.

The threat of losing their families, their positions, and the respect of those who follow them isn't enough to keep them from slipping into destructive behavior. Though I was rescued from pornography and sexual addiction before I was ever caught making such a horrible mistake, I will not say I am above such sin. I have felt the ugly darkness consume me. I have done things I swore I would never do. I have given myself to the beast within, and been lead by its every command. I have been its slave.

The only thing separating me from these men whom I've seen exposed publicly is the grace of God. It could have been me. I know this is true, and it drives me to share my story. I want the world to know there is hope. God wants to deliver us. He has provided a way to be forgiven and practical steps to overcome any addiction or sinful habit.

I have tasted freedom. I have breathed in the fresh air of forgiveness and mercy. Now God has called me to cry out to those who are still held captive. He has called me to share the truth of His love. God has called me to share my story so others will know how they too can break free.

My Calling

Everyone has a special gift. Everyone is created to serve a purpose. Everyone has a reason they exist.

I was created to be a minister. I knew it and fought it for about fourteen years. The draw of preaching never went away but lay dormant. As the years went by, we would drift in and out of church. Along the way I tried resisting my sinful habit, but I was never able to remain in control. The whole time I was drawn to God, but our priorities were off. We would stop going to church or spend all summer going to the lake without once taking time to worship.

I also realized surrendering to preach would mean a huge life change. My family wasn't ready for that. I was not ready for that. Besides, at that point in my life I was not the kind of person you would want as a preacher. I was living a double life, and I praise God for keeping me out of the pulpit and away from the ministry.

After high school graduation I went to college to study education. I planned to be a teacher and coach like my Dad. Val and I set up house in a small apartment near the campus, and we both worked in fast food restaurants to pay the bills. We had mapped out our life together, and were off to a good start. I was going to get my degree and start my career, and then we were going to add to our family. Things were going pretty well, until Val started getting sick.

We were both just eighteen years old and pretty clueless. It never crossed our minds that Val might get pregnant. After all, that was not part of our plan. But just a few weeks into the second semester of my freshmen year, we found out we were going to be parents. We were overwhelmed, scared, and broke. Life would never be the same.

I dropped out of school and went to work selling plots for a realest developer at a nearby lake. After three months I had earned only $300 dollars. We were in a mess. When the electricity was turned off at the apartment I finally called home and asked for help. Mom and Dad were great. They never insulted us or said "I told you so." Instead, they talked to us, gave us a couple of options, and then let us decide what we wanted to do. I will be forever grateful for their help and understanding.

We chose to move back home, and to live with Val's parents until our baby was born. I got a job rebuilding irrigation pumps, and she prepared for the big day. After our little girl was born we rented our own small house and started pursuing a different dream.

As time passed I moved up in the irrigation company and developed a desire to own my own business. My boss was gracious enough to work with me and helped me to develop some business skills. He promoted me to manager of another small service company he owned, and we worked out a deal in which I was supposed to eventually buy the small enterprise from him.

Along the way I was constantly reminded of the urge to minister. Everytime my family would get involved in a church, I would feel the desire surge. I knew one day I would preach, yet I wouldn't give in. I had my own plans, my own dreams. I wanted to own my own company and wanted to be financially independent.

It was not meant to be. Before I was able to accumulate enough savings to make a down payment, my boss sold the business. My whole world was turned upside down. All my plans evaporated in one conversation. I thought I had it all worked out, the company was going to be mine. Now I had six months to train the new owners.

In all fairness, I must let you know my boss did me a great favor. Not only did he give me a generous severance package, but he saved me from making a huge mistake. I have come to understand I am not a gifted business man. That is not my calling. I doubt the company would have lasted a year without his insight and direction. I was a fair manager, but would have never been able to make it work as he did. I now consider this turn of events as a great moment in my life, though at the time it was hard to see it that way.

Those next six months were difficult. I couldn't find a job that paid near what I had been making, and nothing had the promises of ownership and independence. I searched, but never found anything that seemed to fit who I was. Once my time was up, I took a job that really didn't suit me, but it was the best I could find. I was miserable, I didn't last two weeks.

We wound up in Lubbock, where I took a different job. Not long after we moved there, a fellow whom Val worked with invited us to a church in a nearby small town in which he lived. We both knew we needed to go back to church; so we began to attend regularly. The longer we attended and the more involved we became, the greater the urge to minister grew. I could no longer deny I felt drawn to surrender my life to serve God as a preacher. The call was just too strong.

About the same time, Dad had a brain aneurysm. It was a life changing event for my family and me. It was a time of reflection and contemplation. It was the eye opener we needed. It was a blessing from God! Dad survived and fully recovered but not without making a lasting impact on my entire family. It was time to grow up. It was time to change. It was time to pursue God.

Shortly after Dad's brush with death I began to seriously deal with the call to the ministry. Val really wasn't crazy about the idea and quite frankly I was scared to death. It was a bigger challenge than I wanted to take on, and it would mean a great deal of change in our lives. We resisted. We fought. We struggled. Through it all Val and I examined our lives, our marriage, and our dreams. We were forced to ask ourselves the hard questions; did we want to stay married? Could we make such a big adjustment? Was changing our lives really worth it? There were lots of tears shed and plenty of sleepless nights, but a decision had to be made.

I surrendered all one Sunday morning. I couldn't resist the call. I gave myself to the ministry. I pledged my life to serve God by serving others.

I will not lie and say God took away all the trials and temptations. I will not lie and say my family wholly supported me from the get go. I will not lie and say it was pain-free or that Val and I never talked about calling it quits. It was a complicated and painful time. I truly don't know how we survived. Our finances, our marriage, our whole life nearly came apart, but instead of destroying us it matured us and gave us a greater appreciation for all we had. The hard times seem to do that.

My calling as a minister has been the second most difficult part of my life. It has placed a great deal of stress in my marriage and other relationships. It changed our lifestyles and priorities. It has not always been easy, but I know it is what God created me to be. It is my life's purpose.

Through these trials and hardships, Vallarie and I have grown up and learned to lean on God and each other. We also learned to communicate, to be honest with one another, and to forgive. These experiences have made us who we are today.

Freedom?

The addiction was still there. I had not taken a position as a minister yet but knew that was the direction I was headed. Shortly after I surrendered to preach I was confronted with the fact I was still addicted to pornography. God made it very clear to me through a passage in the Bible I had to deal with the problem or I would not be able to fulfill my calling. 2 Timothy 2:20-22 jumped out of scripture and began to change my life. I knew I had to fight with all of my heart, soul, and mind.

I can recall the last time I looked at internet-pornography. We lived in a small duplex. The computer was in our daughter's room. I was home alone and couldn't resist the urge to look. I had slipped back into the addiction despite having surrendered to preach. Each time I would give in I felt more dirty and ashamed. There was no way to hide the truth. I knew I had a serious problem and had been praying and seeking the strength to stop.

God answered my prayer. I guess the answer had been there the whole time but I had refused to listen. This time, He got my attention.

As I was clicking through the images I began to smell a foul odor. I didn't recognize the pungent odor but had a deep feeling within me God was saying something. He revealed to my heart the images were a stench in His nose. He was disgusted by pornography and sexual impurity and was calling me to reject it all because it is offensive to Him. I understood. I finally could see my struggle was more than just a bad habit. I finally understood my choices had real consequences.

I had no more excuses. It was clear deep within my soul that I was offending God and that He would not tolerate my sin. My calling, my marriage, and my children's futures were hanging in the balance. It was time to decide. Would I throw it all away for a few moments of selfishness? Would I walk away from everything just to have an occasional thrill? God brought me to a moment of crisis. Which would I choose?

I had known all along looking at pornography was a sin, but I had put up a wall by justifying my actions and minimizing the affects. I understood the whole time what it was doing to my marriage. Yet I ignored the constant conviction and warnings. I had numbed my conscience to the truth. I had hardened my heart. I was selfish and didn't want to let go of it all. Now, I could see clearly I was literally choosing lust over God and my marriage.

Suddenly, I was overwhelmed with dread and fear. I was sick to my stomach. The seriousness of it all pressed down on me. Would I seek Him, or would I give myself to my habit?

This was a moment of truth, a turning point. I knew I had to fight the temptation with all I had. I began to see that everything I did, every moment of every day, really mattered to God. I knew I had to be changed, transformed from within. I knew my life, my family, and my calling depended on it.

Because of 2 Timothy 2:20-22, I finally understood I had to make a choice. If I was going to serve God and be the man He called me to be then I had to let go of pornography. I couldn't live in impurity and serve Him fully. I couldn't live a double life and be the minister He had created me to be. I couldn't continue to seek my own selfish pleasure and have the kind of marriage God intended for Val and me. I had to face the ugly darkness within. I couldn't hide it any longer.

I guess this was one of those moments when you know you are running out of time. I felt as if this were my one chance to finally change. I cannot fully explain all the thoughts and emotions that were running through my heart and mind. There was an awaking in my soul. God had given me an opportunity to serve Him but I was going to have to do something about my addiction. The time for action had come.

For so long I told myself I would never be free. I couldn't imagine a life without pornography and self-gratification. All my life I had listened to voices that told me I was hopeless and that I would always "need" porn. The darkness held me captive.

Up to this moment I never expected to walk in freedom. I had resigned myself to the fact I was going to remain addicted for the rest of my life. My only hope was to just control it and try my best to keep it from destroying my family and me. I didn't believe I would ever let it go. To be honest, up to that point in life, I probably never wanted to let it go.

But something was different this time. I didn't know how I was going to do it, but I resolved in my heart to change. I vowed to fight against my struggle each day. I knew I had to come clean with Val and ask for her help. I also decided to look for answers in the Bible to find ways to fight back.

2 Timothy 2:20-22 was God's chosen passage for transformation;

> *"[20] Now in a large house there are not only gold and silver vessels, but also vessels of wood and of earthenware, and some to honor and some to dishonor. [21] Therefore, if anyone cleanses himself from these things, he will be a vessel of honor, sanctified, useful to the Master, prepared for every good work. [22] Now flee from youthful lust and pursue righteousness, faith, love and peace, with those who call on the Lord from a pure heart."*

As I studied these verses I could see God had created me with a purpose in mind. Yet at that time I was not a vessel of honor. Instead, I was completely unusable for honorable things. God made it clear to me that unless I fled from the lust, I would never be a vessel of honor.

Basically, the Lord showed me that if I hoped to minister and serve Him and to accomplish the works He had planned for me, I would have to find a way to live in purity. God had a plan from my life, a plan that involved doing good things for His kingdom, but I was preventing it all by giving myself to lust. God pointed out I was living in sin and He wouldn't allow me to fulfill my calling if I chose to remain in sin. The lust was alienating me from God. The lust was preventing my surrender. The lust was quenching the Spirit.

Verse 21 showed me if I would keep myself clean then I would be useful to the Lord, and He could then do good works through me. God had already forgiven me and adopted me as a child, but I was not submitting to His will by "keeping myself clean." This was the problem, and the problem had to be dealt with immediately.

Verse 22 opened my eyes to a life giving truth of God. If I wanted to flee from sin I had to pursue righteousness. In other words, I had to replace my passion for pornography with a passion for godliness. I had to completely change my focus. I couldn't just walk away from lust and expect to remain free. I had to replace it with something else. This is where I had stumbled and came up short every time before. For so long I had seen the need to flee from the sin, but had never replaced it with the pursuit of God. I would try to remain pure, but had nothing else to hold on to. Therefore, the allure of pornography was able to easily pull me back into the shadows, but if I could grab a hold of God's word and plan for my life, then He would rescue me and use me for good. This was a tremendous revelation, perhaps the most significant one in my battle to overcome my struggle. A flicker of hope suddenly appeared in the darkness.

It hasn't been easy, but I have learned to take steps to avoid temptations. I am not free from the affects and allure of the addiction any more than an alcoholic is free from his dependency, but I can take steps to avoid the triggers. I have come to understand the power of making good choices; decisions that prevent me from slipping back into pornography. God is setting me free and I am learning to do my part to receive the freedom. This is the combination that is working. God is doing His part, just as He promised He would all along. Now, I have joined Him in the fight.

The next few chapters express the intense battle that occurred within me as I fought against my addiction. I hope they can somehow help you see how God helped me to face the darkness within me. I pray they spark hope within your own soul.

Facing the Beast

God has always wanted me to take a stand and fight with Him. He has wanted me to suit up and join Him in the battle. He has been there the whole time, waiting, guiding, and urging me on. He has been there, but I never wanted to do it His way. I was more willing to live in the shame and guilt and pain than to fight for freedom.

Sure I wanted to be free, to a certain extent. But to be free meant to let go and to give up something I hated but truly enjoyed at the same time. I knew God's way wouldn't be easy and it would mean a total rejection of my sexual escapades. It was a price I was unwilling to pay for too many years. Though I hated the person I was inside, I didn't want to live my life without pornography. I simply enjoyed it too much. I feared I would miss out on the thrill and excitement it brought me for so long.

I guess all along I understood this, I just wasn't willing to let go. I was trapped. My hate of the addiction wasn't greater than the thrill and pleasure pornography brought into my life. Anyone who has ever been addicted to drugs, alcohol, or anything else probably understands where I am coming from. Though I could see my life beginning to unravel and I knew I was risking everything, I just couldn't stop. The addiction controlled me. I was its slave! I obeyed its demands and sought after its promises of pleasure. Lust controlled me.

It took me years to admit this. For so long I just couldn't confess that I had an addiction. Certainly I knew I was wrong. Certainly I knew I was hurting Val and risking our marriage. Yes, I even knew I was living in sin and that I was going deeper and deeper into a dark world. But I liked it.

To top it off, to admit I couldn't control my desires was a sign of weakness. To admit pornography was controlling me was to admit I wasn't in control. For some reason I wasn't willing to do that. I preferred to justify my actions so I could continue to seek selfish pleasure. Though I hated the inner conflict it caused, I didn't want to let go of my struggle.

Then something changed. The word of God moved me. The passage in the Bible that helped me was Genesis 32:24-32. Our preacher spoke on this text and it changed my life.

In this story Jacob was confronted by God. All his life Jacob had justified his actions and run away from the truth. He was a liar, a scoundrel, and a double crosser. Yet God had chosen him to do mighty things. God had big plans for Jacob, but first, He had to get his attention, so God sent a man to wrestle with Jacob.

That night Jacob and the messenger from God were locked in a battle. At dawn Jacob asked the man to let him go, but he refused to do so until Jacob would tell him his name. Our preacher then pointed out that Jacob's name meant "heal catcher" or "supplanter." This of course was referring to the fact Jacob had "supplanted" or taken the place of his brother Esau wrongly. Through trickery and deceit, Jacob had stolen the blessings that truly belong to his older brother. (Genesis 27:30-38)

As our pastor spoke, God hit me square in the eyes with the truth. I was a pornographer! Until that day I had never admitted this to God or anyone else. Yes, I had admitted that I looked at pornography, but I had never openly confessed I was a pornographer. The title brought chills to my heart.

This moment was vital in my transformation. Up until this point, I had made excuses, justified my actions, blamed others, or just flat out ignored my conscience. I couldn't any longer. The Spirit of God fully convicted me of my sin. He made it painfully clear I was full of lust and selfishness.

I wrestled with God that day, so to speak. I, like Jacob, wanted to be blessed and used for mighty works. But at that point I was not a vessel of honor. I was not in a place in which God could bless me or use me for good works. I was a pornographer.

So like Jacob, I declared my name. I openly confessed to my Lord who I was and what I had done. I poured out my heart, and begged for His mercy, knowing I had nothing within me that deserved forgiveness. I could not rely on my own goodness or accomplishments. All I could trust in was His love and His grace.

After being confronted and awakened by 2 Timothy 2:20-22 and Genesis 32:24-32, I finally faced the beast with in me and confessed my sins before God. I admitted my addiction and selfish love of pornography. I told God I enjoyed looking at porn, even though I knew it was wrong and offensive in His eyes. I admitted to God I had chosen to obey lust instead of Him. I faced the ugliness of my own desires, and then asked God to forgive me and purify me.

I cried out for mercy because I had read over and over in the Bible He is kind, compassionate, and ready to forgive those who fear Him and seek His grace. I believed this was true for years but never completely took that step. Instead, I tried to contain my struggle under my own power. Sure I would ask God to forgive me after I would slip into sin, but I never faced the beast. In other words: I never laid it all out before Him at one time. I never admitted my love for the pleasure. All I had really wanted was for Him to take away the guilty feelings.

This time it was different; I was honest, real, and willing to tell God I really enjoyed it all, even though it offended Him. I stopped trying to hide the way it made me feel and quit lying to myself that I didn't have a serious problem. I admitted I was choosing sin and selfish pleasure over Him. That was hard but it was true.

I also finally confessed to Val all I had done. I broke down and begged for forgiveness. Until then, I justified lying to her by telling myself I was protecting her. In reality, I was only trying to protect myself. In the end, I only caused her more pain.

I hurt her deeply. Time after time I had told her I'd stopped. She had no idea what I faced, the depth of my addiction. I was so careful to keep it all hidden, which only made it worse. The longer I kept it inside the tighter pornography gripped me. Instead of reaching out for help, I tried to fight it all myself and the beast nearly consumed me and it caused her more pain in the long run.

That evening as we yelled, cried, held each other, and spoke honestly, something happened. I was relieved. The darkness that had set for so long upon my soul was gone. It was as if a huge weight had been lifted off my shoulders. I was clean.

Once I was finally able to admit how much I really enjoyed pornography, I was headed in the right direction. As long as I denied its power over me and ran from the truth, I was unable to break free. I had to face the beast if I hoped to slay it.

Val was so vital. She was strong enough to confront me and hold me accountable. Yet she was compassionate and forgiving too. I needed both. God used her to help me see just how ugly my struggle was. She still doesn't understand how much she helped me.

One of the most valuable things she provided was accountability. She loved me enough and hated the pornography enough to not let it just slip by. She confronted me, forced me to be honest, and prayed for me and with me.

With her help the beast was exposed. The darkness was brought to light. In the light- the light of God- the ugliness was clear. In the light, I could deal with the sinfulness of it all. In the light, I could finally be honest with Val and most importantly, honest with myself. The more God showed me, the more I wanted to be transformed. I no longer wanted to just cover up the sin. I truly wanted to be free and to never let it consume me again.

I guess the best way to describe it is this; for the first time I sincerely wanted to never look at pornography again because I understood how vile and disgusting and dangerous it was. Until that moment I simply wanted to never get caught, to not feel guilt and shame, and to be able to live with myself, all without giving up the pleasure that porn and self-gratification brought into my life. I wanted to be able to continue in sin without facing the consequences. That is honestly why I never let go. That was the reality of it all.

When I faced this and confessed it before God and Val, I was able to move forward. The urges remained, but the motivation of my heart had shifted. That is when everything began to change.

Once the beast was exposed I could begin to fight with truth. I could swing the sword of God's word at the monster that lived within me. It wasn't always comfortable or easy, but I began to win the battle. My eyes were opened. I was able to see the damage it had caused, and I caught a glimpse of the potential outcome. I didn't want to lose my family. I didn't want to destroy my marriage. I didn't want to throw away all God had blessed me with. At the same time I could see a glimmer of hope. I began to believe in the possibility of never going back. Slowly I became more able to ward off temptations. Gradually I began to desire purity more than selfish, instant pleasure. I had tasted freedom, and I wanted out of the prison I finally realized I was in.

Walking with God

God always had the answers. God knew what I needed and He truly wanted to set me free all along. Yet I always turned away. I had been rejecting all of His help and the fullness of His power and love. I didn't want His help because I didn't really want to let go. Up to that point I had chosen pornography over freedom. I had chosen sin over obedience.

Once I understood just how much damage my addiction was causing and that I was close to disaster, I was able to take a stand. The Bible is pretty clear about obedience and turning from "youthful lust." There is no doubt in God's word about the clear commandments to flee from sexual immorality. Yet I had never really let the truth penetrate my heart. I kept it at bay. I never wanted to read about or study in depth the warnings and commands about sex. To do so would have meant I would have to confront the beast. That would have caused pain and discomfort and I certainly didn't want to go there. The answer was available all along. I just refused to let God work within me.

Once I began to grow deeper in my knowledge of God, I grew to love the truth and power of His word. As this happened I began to crave purity. Along the way I began to understand obedience leads to God's favor and blessings; I started wanting to walk with God and not to just simply fulfill my own desires. I began to see the payoff for a moment of pleasure could never compare to the richness of obeying Him.

Along the way, I found my greatest weapons of deliverance were God's word, prayer, obeying the Holy Spirit, and accountability. These elements have been so vital in my walk to freedom. When I slip in any of these areas I begin to face growing temptations and the allure of our society's obsession with sex. I must stay focused by reading the Bible, praying sincerely and constantly, responding to the whispers of God, and by talking to Val and my friends honestly. I praise God for these key elements in my transformation.

This is nothing new. The Bible is full of examples as to how God uses these exact things to change and empower His people. For so long I just simply refused to fight the battle His way. I wanted to take the easy way out. I wanted to try to live half my life as a Christian and the other half in sin. Finally, through His word, God showed me this simply wouldn't work.

He helped me to see if I wanted to serve Him, to have a solid family life, to live without guilt and shame, and to grow in my relationship with Him, then I was going to have to make some changes. God showed me I couldn't serve two masters; so I chose to submit to Him. This is the same choice millions of others have made. King David, Daniel, Peter, and Paul made the same decision. In fact Joshua 24:14-15 boldly puts that very question before us. Will we serve God? Will we choose today to make Him our Lord? It's a real choice, which produces real results, one way or the other.

One of the revelations that has shaped me greatly and helped me to pursue God is the truth that following God is good for me. This may seem simplistic at first, but it is a truth that has changed my life. For so long I didn't want to walk with God because I thought it would make my life miserable, boring, and too "goody-goody." I had this image in my head of a Christian life, and what it would be like, and quite frankly it was not very attractive.

At the time if someone would have said, "Choose today whom you will serve," I would have probably taken option "B." The idea of going to church, reading the Bible, avoiding sin, and telling others about Jesus completely turned me off. I wanted a life filled with excitement and adventure, thrills and pleasures. The last thing I wanted was to turn out to be a stuffy old Christian.

But as I studied the Bible and came into contact with amazing Christian people I began to see my idea of Christianity was wrong. Somehow I had bought into the lie that being a Christian was a rotten way to have to live. I had been deceived and had rejected the best way of living and had accepted a cheap imitation. I was seeking a counterfeit life, filled with counterfeit pleasures.

Once God opened my eyes to the truth, I began to hunger for a better life. I wanted to stop living in guilt and shame. I wanted to experience the kind of life the Bible promises for those who follow Him. I wanted to live in freedom. I guess I finally began to see that God's ways are better than my own.

My grandmother gave me a scripture once that helped me to see this more clearly. Jeremiah 33:3 gave me a thirst to experience God like never before.

> *"Call to Me and I will answer you, and I will tell you great and mighty things, which you do not know."*

I wanted to see and hear great and mighty things. I wanted to learn more about God. I knew deep inside it would change me.

Also Jeremiah 29:11 and Romans 8:28 began to shape my way of thinking. I began to see if God loved me, was all powerful, had good plans for my life, and wanted to bless me, then perhaps I needed to give myself to Him completely. I could see the possibilities of being favored and blessed by God and it sounded good. I could see there was far greater potential in a life that was pleasing to God versus a life that was lived in opposition to His commandments. I could finally see a few moments of pleasure were not worth being outside the will of God.

These truths changed me. Somehow deep within my soul a desire to walk with God was born. As I tasted the goodness of His love and blessings, I found I wanted for more. A thirst for doing things His way began to replace my thirst for selfish pleasure.

I am certainly not perfect. I still find myself tempted from time to time. So I must be quick to confess and quick to seek God's help through the Holy Spirit, His word, and prayer. I have also needed the help of accountability from Val and my friends. Yet by His grace and my devotion, I have great hope and peace and have experienced life in abundance. (John 10:10) Today I thirst for more and still believe His way is the only way to enjoy life to the fullest.

I have come to understand my sex drive is part of who I am. It will always be a part of my story. Therefore, I will never say I am above a relapse. But God has given me the great opportunity to be set free from lust. I can walk daily in His love and power, and I can overcome. To do so I must obey. I must live by His word. Yet freedom and purity are possible. To top it off, I have learned that submitting my sexual desires to Him actually is much more beneficial too. My marriage has grown, and my relationship with Val has flourished. Our sex life is better than ever, and our communication is wonderful. The enemy tried to destroy these things and to steal our joy. He almost won. But God rescued us and restored the gift of sex and intimacy. They are blessing our marriage and knitting us together, just as He intended all along. His ways are better!

Walking with God has changed my life. Since God has begun to set me free I have been able to speak openly and frankly about my struggle. This has been helpful because I no longer hide in the darkness. I am ashamed of the past and the choices I made, but I find joy in the knowledge that God has transformed my soul. He has done an amazing work within me, and I believe He wants to do the same work in anyone who is facing his own struggle. God wants to set us all free so we can all live life to the fullest.

Prison

I lived a great part of my life in a prison. My body and mind craved sexual stimulation and pleasure. I was drawn deeper and deeper into a world of darkness. At the same time my heart and soul cried out for help. Within me a battle raged. I wanted to be a nice guy. I wanted to obey God. I wanted to honor my marriage vows. Yet I also wanted to experience the thrills and pleasures I had seen and heard portrayed so many times.

I didn't choose to have to face this struggle. I never wanted to head down a road of heartache and pain. Yet that was the road I was on. The influences and choices I made as a child and teenager led me astray and the constant desire to experience sexual pleasure held me captive.

Many times I vowed to myself, to Val, and even to God, to never indulge again. At the time I meant it. I hated the way pornography and lust controlled me. I hated the look of hurt and disappointment and disgust in Val's eyes. I hated the dirty and sick feeling each time I gave in. Yet it seemed I would never find freedom.

The Bible has helped me understand this struggle. Romans 6:16 is one example of a Bible verse that touched my soul.

"Do you not know that when you present yourselves to someone as slaves for obedience, you are slaves of the one whom you obey, either sin resulting in death, or of obedience resulting in righteousness?"

Through this scripture, I can see now that I continually submitted myself to pornography and lust. I gave myself to be their slave. I surrendered my will so I could enjoy a few moments of sexual fulfillment and excitement. Pornography and lust were my masters. I obeyed the desires they instilled. I sought after their promised rewards. I bowed to their demands. They, in a sense, were my gods.

I am not alone. Romans 7:14-25 is Paul's expression of the very same prison I found myself in. Paul, the amazing Apostle of Christ, found himself trapped by sin as well. (I am not suggesting Paul struggled with lust because we do not know specifically what he is referring to here. What we do know is he had a problem with sin, just like you and me.) The fact that Paul had a struggle with sin has brought me great comfort and hope. If Paul, this amazing man of God, faced a struggle then maybe there was a chance God could use me too.

God's word has shown me I am not alone. God truly knows how I feel and He wants to help me break free. You may feel trapped as well. Your struggle may not be pornography. Perhaps you cannot stop drinking alcohol. Maybe you have a problem with gambling. Or your struggle may be trying to look like a London fashion model.

You probably know the battle that rages within. That deep desire to do right but at the same time a deep desire to do what you know is wrong and harmful. You fight. You try to do what is good, but all along you know it is just a matter of time before you take a drink, place a bet, or throw up again. You hate yourself. You hate your struggle, but it controls you.

You ask yourself over and over again, when will I finally get it right? When will I finally stop? Why won't God just take it all away? If He loves me so much why does He let me hurt? Why won't He just make it stop!

I asked those questions hundreds of times. I finally found the answer. Romans 6:17-18 has opened up the truth and brought me wisdom. There has to be a change within us. Something has to break. We have to move from obeying the darkness into obeying the light. We have to have a new master. We have to bow to a new god, the true God!

It would be a lie to say this is simple and pain-less. It would be a lie to say all it takes is one simple prayer. It would be a lie to say I have the magic phrase or insight to make it all go away, there is no such thing.

The truth is you must crucify that part of you, the darkness; the one thing you hate but love. (Colossians 3:5-7) I hope you are caught off guard by the word crucify. It is an ugly word. It describes a brutal act of death. It is painful. It is bloody. But it is the only way.

Let me expound on this a little. You cannot play nicely with your darkness. You cannot let it remain an option. You cannot just tuck it away in the back corner of your mind and hope it will leave you alone. You must destroy it. You must crucify it! Isn't that the message of Mark 9:47?

"If your eye causes you to stumble, throw it out; it is better for you to enter the kingdom of God with one eye, than, having two eyes, to be cast into hell."

If sin is causing you to stumble, take action! Don't tolerate sin in your life. Take drastic steps to eliminate temptation. God is not asking us to literally mutilate our bodies, but He is using an exaggeration to make a point: act now, do something about your sinful habits!

For example, I cannot allow myself to dabble on internet sites that are questionable. If I see a site contains any type of sexual content, I must quickly close the page. If I am watching television and a beer commercial full of scantly clad women comes on, I must change the channel, leave the room, or look away. You get the idea. I must take real and deliberate actions to defend my desire to live in purity. I must make a purposeful choice to avoid temptation. This is doing my part to fight with God for my freedom.

I am not saying that if I see a half-naked woman suddenly I will fall back into an uncontrollable addiction to pornography. What I am saying is that everything I see and listen to makes a difference, and I refuse to give the devil a foothold once again. I refuse to play with fire.

Now you may think this is extreme, but I promise you it is vital. Job made a covenant with his eyes to never look lustfully on a woman. (Job 31:1-4) He understood the danger of allowing his eyes to linger upon a woman. He could see the danger of letting his mind wonder or of letting a fantasy grow. He made a vow to look away, to close his eyes, or to do whatever he had to in order to keep from falling into lust.

This passage in the Bible also reveals Job believed God was watching and that He was the ultimate Judge. Job understood that every thought he had mattered to God. Job understood that even if his wife or friends did not see, God did! Job took this very seriously. Perhaps that is why God could proclaim Job was a "blameless and upright man, fearing God and turning away from evil." (Job 1:8)

This was a truth that came to life for me in 2 Timothy 2:20-22. I began to see that everything I did mattered to God. Furthermore, my actions, my thoughts, and my choices would have a direct impact on God's hand in my life. God's blessings and favor are greatly influenced by my willingness to obey Him.

I have come to a greater understanding of this fact throughout the past few years. God is my judge. God knows my heart, my desires, and every single thing I do. I cannot hide a glance, a click, or a thought. God is aware of everything I do or say or think.

Also, my ability to serve God, my relationship to my family, God's favor and blessings, and my eternal rewards all hinge on my willingness to obey Him. The Bible is very clear about our responsibility to obey God's word. We cannot ignore the Old and New Testament teachings about this truth. What we do matters, and God demands our faithfulness. God also rewards those who seek Him. (Hebrews 11:6)

Please let me stress the fact we are not saved (given eternal life) by our works. Ephesians 2:8-9 quickly proves this fact.

> *"⁸For by grace you have been saved through faith; and that not of yourselves, it is the gift of God; ⁹not as a result of works, so that no one my boast."*

God doesn't forgive our sins and give us the promise of eternal life based on our ability to follow His commands. We are forgiven and blessed with eternal life only by His grace when we respond in faith to the message of Jesus Christ. Otherwise, we would be hopeless. We can never earn His love or forgiveness. If we could in any way earn our salvation then Jesus died needlessly for we could have saved ourselves. (Galatians 2:15-21)

Salvation is absolutely free. God will forgive anyone and give them eternal life when they sincerely believe and cry out for His mercy and love. (Romans 10:9-13) Again, we are saved solely by placing our faith in Jesus Christ, not by obeying His commands.

However, our life on earth and our eternity are greatly shaped by our obedience as children of God. Our choices, our willingness to obey God, and our deeds have a direct impact both here on earth and in eternity. (Luke 18:28-30)

This reality has greatly shaped my life. It has helped me surrender my sexual desires. It has helped me obey God even when my body and mind wanted to do otherwise. It has taught me that it is always worth it to honor God in everything I do.

I also believe it has had a lasting impact on my wife and children. For example, if I had not stepped away from pornography, I believe Val and I would probably have been divorced by now. This would have greatly changed not only mine and Vallarie's life, but more so our daughters'. Furthermore, I would have been a different dad. My daughters needed a godly dad who was willing to obey God and lead them in the right direction. I wasn't doing that when I was trapped in sin. Instead, my focus was on myself and my own desires. I praise God my priorities have changed.

Obeying God and seeking Him have also allowed me to be a minister. As I stated earlier, I don't believe God would have allowed me to pastor had I not surrendered to His will. I could have taken a job as a minister, but the truth would have come out and I can only imagine what the outcome would have been, the damaged it would have caused, the shame and embarrassment that would have ensued.

Likewise, had I refused to conform to His will, I would have missed out on all He has done in my life through the ministry. My family and I would have never known the fullness of His love and faithfulness.

God has greatly blessed my family and me, but we have not earned these blessings. Changing our lives has simply put us in a place that allows God to bless us. Matthew 6:33 is a great example of how obeying God and seeking His will enables Him to meet our needs.

"But seek first His kingdom and His righteousness, and all these things will be added to you."

He has promised to take care of us and has proved Himself faithful. I could not even begin to explain all of the ways He has met our needs through various people and circumstances. Yet had I continued to submit to pornography, I doubt we would have ever experienced the wonderful gifts He has poured out over us in the past few years.

Up until the time I surrendered I had been living within a prison, I had missed out on the possibilities that come through doing things God's way. It is kind of like being literally held in a jail cell. You not only have to spend your days in confinement, but you also miss the joys of freedom.

Psalm 107:10-16 is a vivid description of my life. I have been a "prisoner in misery and chains." But I have also tasted the sweet grace of God who responded when I "cried out to the Lord." The prison door has been blown wide open, and I want to continue to walk in freedom. I never want to go back.

Your Struggle

We all have struggles. We all have battles that seem to consume us or transform our lives. I have tried to share my struggle in hopes you too may be able to overcome and find freedom. Whatever your struggle, you can find hope. Whatever you battle, you can be free from its control. God wants to open the prison gates and allow you to walk out of the darkness. He wants to bless you and do amazing things in your life.

You probably already know what has defined your life. You probably know all to well what has held you captive for too long. Perhaps like me, you have found sexuality as a life-long struggle. Maybe you battle a drug addiction or alcoholism. You may fight against depression or low self-esteem. Your struggle might be less "dramatic" and harder to define. It could be a desire for recognition that controls you. Maybe it is a desire to have the finer things in life. Whatever you face, it is no less daunting or dangerous.

Jealousy, greed, envy, gossip, fear, depression, or some other "prison" may hold you captive. No matter what it is, you can be delivered! God wants to help you climb out of the pit. God wants to open the gates of your private prison cell. He wants to set you free.

If you hope to find freedom you must take the first step: identify your struggle. Liberty must start at knowing your prison. Freedom begins when you can honestly see what holds you in chains. You must identify your enemy, your struggle.

Call it what it is. We often hide behind lies and false realities. Instead of facing our struggle and admitting it has a hold on our lives, we choose to live in bondage. There is nothing worse in life than giving in to slavery and captivity. I have seen middle-aged adults and even senior citizens who were never able to break free. They are hopeless and empty. The light of life has vanished from their eyes. They have submitted to slavery and believe that is all life has to offer. It is a sad and painful way to live, but you don't have to live that way. You don't have to remain in prison. There is hope!

Just as God has opened my eyes and helped me face my struggle, you, too, can find forgiveness, hope, and power. God is on your side. He wants to set you free.

The first step has to be confessing the truth. What do you struggle with? What holds you back? Fear? Lust? Greed? Guilt? An addiction? If a messenger from God was to ask you what your "name" is, what would you say?

If you are unsure, pray and ask God to help you see. He will expose your struggle. When He does bring it to the light, don't let it hold you captive any longer. Call it what it is. Face the beast and let the healing begin.

When young David arrived on the scene in 1 Samuel 17, he could clearly see who the enemy was. The giant mocked God and held the entire army of Israel at bay. David was enraged and set out to kill the enemy. The battle lines were clearly drawn. The enemy was evident. Goliath didn't stand a chance!

Years later David had a little more trouble identifying the enemy. He had sent the troops off to fight, but he stayed back for some rest and relaxation. In the process David spotted a woman bathing on her roof. We know where all of this led and how the king not only committed adultery but murder as well. (2 Samuel 11)

This time David could not identify the enemy; so God sent Nathan in to expose the "giant." (2 Samuel 12:1-15) The prophet tells David a story about a rich man who steals a poor man's lamb. The king is furious and orders the rich man to be executed. David is unaware that he is pronouncing judgment on himself. The enemy was not quite so evident this time.

In verse seven of this passage Nathan tells the king, "You are that man." God sent the prophet to show David the enemy was within him. The beasts of lust and murder were so close David couldn't identify them. Has this ever happened to you?

For so long a beast lurked within me. I knew something was there but never really faced it or called it what it was. Finally, God showed me I had to face the beast and call it by its name. Once I did, I was able to fight against the enemy and draw strength from specific revelations in God's word.

This is the first step in your battle to overcome your struggle. You must know what you are fighting against. You must identify who you are and what weaknesses you have. Have you taken this step? Have you faced the monster and called it by its name? In my case it was "lust." That is what it all boiled down to. The pornography and self-indulgence were both results of the lust within me. Once I could call it by its name and could see clearly what I was fighting against, I could amass weapons of war to attack the beast.

If you hope to break free you are going to have to identify the enemy. What holds you captive? What is your struggle?

I must warn you, it is not easy to slay the beast. Why? Because in some strange way the monster within, the habit that holds you captive, is familiar and you have grown attached to it. The best way I can describe it is that the beast is like an old friend. This was the way I felt. I knew pornography was hurting me. I knew it was sinful and causing pain in my life. I knew it could destroy all I cherished, but I was attached to porn.

Remember, I began this struggle when I was eight years old. Pornography had been a part of my life for over twenty years: longer than any friendship, longer than Val and I had been married, longer than I had been a Christian. It was part of who I was, a part of my history and life experience. It was like an old friend.

Walking away from a long-term habit is not easy. Turning from something that has brought you pleasure, comfort, or security is never easy. Sacrificing anything is not a simple or pain-free process, no matter how much you know it is necessary. It is a sacrifice!

Crucifying your habit, your struggle, will involve a sort of "mourning." Even though it is the best thing for you, and it is the best choice you can make, you will probably have a difficult time letting go, just as if you were telling a friend goodbye.

I know people who have hung onto painful, dangerous, and destructive relationships for years. They want out but can't let go. They know they should walk away but just can't seem to find the strength. They hang on, hoping something will change, praying the situation will somehow get better. It's killing them inside, but they just keep hanging on. No matter how many times someone tells them to leave, they don't. No matter how desperately they want to have a better life, they stay trapped. Though they know the relationship is wrong, it is also familiar. Though it is painful, it is comfortable. They are more afraid of letting go and facing the unknown than they are of continuing in pain.

Our addictions often affect us in the same way. We know what we ought to do. We know what is best. We know there is a better way, but we just keep hanging on as it pulls us farther and farther away from the person we truly want to be.

When I finally "faced the beast" and "crucified" my habit, I had to face the reality that I could never go back. I had to let go of my "old friend" and move on. It wasn't easy, but it was one of the best choices I have ever made in my entire life.

Honestly, it took me a while to stop missing pornography. But as a relationship fades over time, so has my affection for porn. My grief has turned into rejoicing. God has filled the empty space with so much more than I could have ever imagined. I am so glad I let go.

The process is not easy, but you can walk away. You can overcome. You can be transformed and enjoy life as God intended it. There is life after addiction. There is freedom from sinful habits. You don't have to remain chained to your struggle any longer.

Unlocking Your Chains

Our struggles imprison us. They lock us up and hold us in bondage. We strain and fight against the chains but only find ourselves exhausted and hopeless and bruised. Many people give up and resign their lives to captivity. They learn to live within the prison and stop longing for freedom. Others fight and struggle for the rest of their lives but are unable to break free. Their lives are filled with misery and regrets.

I know what it is like to be locked in a dungeon, bound to a chain. I know what it is like to strain against the chains that bind our lives. It is lonely. It is frightening. It can steal all of our hope and joy. It can make life miserable.

What can help? Who can set you free? What makes this time any different from the times before?

You must understand you cannot face this darkness alone. You must rely on God and the support of mature Christians. If you want to finally break free you are going to have to do it His way and through

His power. This is not the easy way out, but it is the only way out. Nothing else will work.

God empowers us through His word and the Holy Spirit. If you are a Christian then you have the ability to overcome any addiction. You have the ability to overcome any struggle because you are not alone in this fight.

The Bible teaches us that all Believers have been sealed with the Holy Spirit. (Ephesians 1:13-14, 1 Corinthians 6:18-20) When you believe and confess Jesus as Lord, you are not only forgiven, you are sealed. Your eternal destination is changed and God Himself, through the Holy Spirit, takes up residence within you. This is vital and is truly the first of three keys that will unlock your chains.

Christians, we are not alone. The Holy Spirit of God dwells within you and will empower you, guide you, and comfort you as you fight for freedom. God wants to set you free, and He has provided a Helper. (John 14:16-18) You must embrace this teaching. You must let this fact resound within your heart and soul.

Why is this so important? The truth is: we are weak and powerless. Our human nature holds us back and causes us to stumble in the darkness. It is our human nature that brought us into captivity. (James 1:13-16) It is our human nature that craves darkness. This is the truth of our human existence. You must understand that apart from His help you cannot break free. However, what you have been unable to accomplish on your own is now possible through the power of the Holy Spirit.

Paul understood this truth. Romans 7:14-25 brings this out. Paul had a conflict within his soul. He had a desire to follow God and to live in purity, yet something within him still craved sin. Something within him fought against the Spirit. You may understand this struggle. You probably know what it's like to "practice the very evil I do not want."

He goes on to teach us in Romans 8:1-8 that by ourselves, in our human nature alone, we cannot overcome. In fact, I found the more I fought against temptation and lust under my own power, the more frustrated and trapped I became. As I struggled against the chains they only became tighter! I think I can understand where Paul was coming from.

Yet Paul shares with us that there is hope. Romans 8:9-17 reminds us that Christians have the Holy Spirit and by His power we can be set free. We have been adopted as "Children of God." Therefore, there is hope for those who belong to Him.

This is so vital in your walk to freedom. God is able to show you the way, guide you, convict your heart, and encourage you directly because His Spirit lives within you. Can you see how important this is to you as you pursue freedom?

You are not alone. You have a helper. The Holy Spirit is able to remind you of scripture that will guide you and the Holy Spirit is able to teach you. (John 14:26) Furthermore, you cannot break free without His help. This key is absolutely necessary if you hope to overcome, yet it is so often forgotten or we are never even aware of the Spirit's presence within us.

Have you ever lost your car keys? If so, you know what it is like to desperately search. You tear up your bedroom and living room trying to find them. You flip over the couch cushions and you look under the bed; as the minutes tick by you become more and more frantic and hopeless. Without those keys you cannot go to work, to the store, or to see your friends. The feeling can be overwhelming. Where are those keys!

Then you realize you wore your jacket the night before and had hung it in the closet as you came through the door. Your fear begins to melt away as you calmly reach into your jacket pocket and feel the cold metal meet your fingertips. Suddenly you are at peace. You have the keys in your hand and you head out the door to face the day. The keys were there the whole time. They were within reach all along. This is similar to our lack of awareness of the Holy Spirit within us.

God is there, available, teaching, and guiding us the whole time. However, because we are unaware of His presence, we often miss out on the comfort and strength that is available to us. The key to freedom has been there the whole time while we frantically try to solve our problems ourselves.

The next key is God's word: knowing and obeying God's commands. I know this may seem too simple and probably isn't what you want to hear, but it is the truth and the second key to freedom.

One of the most powerful passages in my life has been Psalm 119:9-16. God wants to set us free and has given us instructions, but we often just simply refuse to learn and apply the truth to our lives. If you want to be free it will come only by abiding in Christ. This is simply obeying the commandments God has laid out for us within the Bible. (John 15:5-11)

I cannot stress enough the importance of learning and living out God's commands. As Psalm 119:9-16 teaches us, if we want to keep our way pure, we must keep it according to His word. There is no other means of freedom. If we fail to seek truth through the Bible we will be led astray, wind up confused, and remain imprisoned.

This may seem like a daunting and impossible task. It really is not. In fact, most of us know the basics of God's word. The problem is: we don't even apply what we currently know. We most often select the commands we are most comfortable with and pretty much ignore the rest. All this does is leave us trapped within the dark cell.

We also need to know the promises of God's word. The Bible is not just a list of do's and don'ts. God has made us amazing promises and we need to know them well. The more I know about the things God has told us He will do, the more I desire to know Him and follow Him. God's promises really reveal His character.

These promises give me hope in my times of need. They encourage me and remind me it is always worth it to invest my life in Christ. We need to be reminded God is faithful and that He desires what is good. The more we learn and grow in His promises the greater our trust in Him becomes. We need to know His word. We need to then apply His word into our lives so our "joy may be made full." (John 15:11)

The third key is prayer. Prayer is basically communication with God. The primary help that prayer provides is the opportunities for us to think about, talk to, and listen to God. There is no magic formula for prayer, other than, sincerity. A sincere prayer is powerful. God responds to authentic prayers.

It is usually in prayer or following a time of prayer that I find my greatest help. I believe it is because I slow down, focus, and think about God and His word. I can claim His promises, remember His warnings, and confess my sins. I can also plea for help, and I am often reminded of His grace and love while praying.

When we fail to pray we miss the opportunity to share our hearts, to focus in on God's revealed will, and to hear His voice. This is one of the great tragedies of our time. We often find ourselves so busy and distracted that we ignore prayer. We make time for chores, television, surfing the web, and a list of other activities, but we neglect one of the most powerful and essential elements of walking in freedom. Then we wonder why we find ourselves trapped and enslaved.

Prayer is not always convenient. Prayer is not always comfortable. Prayer is a spiritual discipline which requires our attention and commitment, but if you hope to walk in freedom, you are going to have to invest some time and energy in prayer.

I wish I could say that the moment you've finished your prayer the answers would come in a loud booming voice. Yet that is not what happens on most occasions. Normally it is gradual. Most of the time, God just reminds me of what He has already taught me, and then He nudges me to obey what I already know is true. Occasionally it is more dramatic than that, but only rarely.

Sometimes He will give me a fresh revelation. Sometimes I feel His presence, but most often it is just an exercise of faith and seeking. I don't always come away with a sure-fire answer, but I know he is listening and that He cares. Overall, the time spent in reflection and focus on Him usually helps me make the right choices.

God is pleased when we seek Him in prayer. (1 Thessalonians 5:17, 2 Chronicles 7:14) He will even help us when we don't know how or what to pray. (Romans 8:26-27) Prayer is such a vital part of our walk with God. It is essential in our search for freedom and recovery.

God has given us clear and proven ways to unlock our chains and to live in freedom. If we will lean on His Holy Spirit, seek Him in prayer, and learn His word and then apply it in our lives, we will begin to feel the chains loosen. The prison door will swing open, and we can walk out of the cell.

His word is powerful and fills us with the truth and gives us practical information to apply to our lives. The Holy Spirit within us will help us learn and apply the word of truth. He will also remind us when we stumble. He will teach us to avoid pitfalls. He will identify areas of weakness, and He will bring us hope through the testimonies and truths within the Bible.

Prayer then helps us focus and opens our hearts to hear what God is saying. It helps us see more clearly. These keys work together. You cannot unlock the chains without using all three keys. We can try, we can tug at the locks, and we can hope the locks will just simply fall off. Or we can take these three keys, unlock the chains, and run to freedom.

This is so important. I know people who want God to do everything. I was that person! I wanted God to simply take way my pain, my struggle, and my shame. I wanted Him to do all the work. I would become angry with God because I didn't understand why He wouldn't just end my suffering. After all, if He loved me, why would He not want me to break free? Why would He not help me? He has the power to do all things, including changing my life, so why should I have to do anything?

This is so common. We are trying to unlock the chains without using the right keys. We believe God is real. We know He has the power and authority and that He is merciful. We have faith but still cannot break free, so we become frustrated and hopeless. In some cases this causes people to turn away from God altogether. I hope this has not happened to you. If it has, I assure you God is there waiting for you to return and seek Him. He wants to set you free.

On the other side of this point, we often get frustrated when we read scripture and find no help or comfort. This could be the result of two things. First, you may not be a Christian. You may know about Jesus but may have never really surrendered your life into His hands. That is not the main topic of this book but can explain why you find no comfort or strength in the words of the Bible. If this is the case, I hope you will give your life to Jesus. I pray you will trust Him as Lord and Savior, and let God seal you with the Holy Spirit.

The second possibility is that you are not allowing the Holy Spirit to direct you. This is also a part of my past. As I wrote earlier, I was saved when I was sixteen. I confessed my sins and asked to be cleansed. I believed Jesus was the Son of God, and that He came to the earth, was born of a virgin, died on the cross, and was raised again on the third day. I trusted in God's word and was given eternal life on that day.

Yet I didn't stop living in sin. I didn't change. Sure I would fight and struggle against the pornography, but I was never really transformed. I read the Bible, but it really didn't seem to make a difference. So I really didn't believe I would ever change.

After I surrendered to the ministry I began to learn more about the Holy Spirit. Our pastor taught us about the empowering part of God that indwells those who are sealed by God. I began to believe I could be different and that God could work within me despite my faults and failures. I learned about being filled by the Spirit by laying aside my own will and following Him. This was a life-giving breath of fresh air. Suddenly I had hope.

I began to trust that God was able to teach me and started to try to apply the words of the Bible, even the words I didn't like. I realized I couldn't take just the easy and comforting parts of God's word and reject the parts I didn't like or fully understand. I began to change. This new understanding of the Holy Spirit was transforming the way I looked at God and His word. It even changed the way I prayed.

It was about this time that God revealed the meaning of 2 Timothy 2:20-22. Suddenly I was aware of the power of purity. I could see the way I lived really did matter and could no longer tolerate being two people. I decided I had to wholeheartedly follow God's plan for my life if I hoped to live in freedom. I couldn't serve God and lust. Only one could be my Master.

As I began to see the power of God's word and grew in my understanding about the Holy Spirit, my life started to change. The things that used to attract me began to become disgusting to me. God was also helping me see how pornography was poisoning my life and harming my family. What I used to crave was now becoming despised in my heart. He began to open my eyes and allowed me to see how pornography and our sexually saturated culture were taking other people captive too. He also helped me to understand that He wouldn't tolerate a little sin here and there. He wanted all of my heart, not just the part I wanted to give Him. These new understandings were transforming me from within.

You, too, can gain new understanding and experience the life-changing power of God. You can be set free from the prison cell that has held you captive for so long. God can and will work within you by the power of His Holy Spirit, His word, and prayer.

Grab hold of the keys, unlock the chains, and walk towards freedom.

The Truth Will Set You Free

I think I can identify the greatest factor in my life that has transformed me and made the biggest difference within me. I finally concluded in my heart, soul, and mind that the Bible is God's word. (2 Timothy 3:16-17) I struggled with this as a teenager and young adult. I wanted to believe but was faced with doubts and questions that no one could answer to my satisfaction. Over the years my doubts faded as my faith increased. The more I believed the Bible was literally "God breathed" and "was useful for teaching, rebuking, correcting, and training in righteousness," the more it changed me.

As my faith in God's word transformed me, I made a choice; the Bible would be my standard. I chose to hold everything else up to the word of God and to judge the rest of life based on the Bible, not vice versa. I believe this has been the most significant change in me and has precipitated in amazing growth and maturity.

This new view of the Bible and holding it as the supreme standard transformed me. There are some basic Biblical truths that I know have changed my life: God loves me no matter what I have done or how bad I have been; God wants to set me free and has given me the Holy Spirit to help me unlock the chains; God has given me very real and specific instructions in the Bible; God will help me, but I must obey and follow Him to find true freedom; God has promised to bless and deliver those who seek Him; God can and will redeem my mistakes and turn evil into good.

These are basic Biblical truths. Most of us know them and would probably agree that these are important, but do we really believe them enough to apply them to our lives? So often I find myself acknowledging these truths in my mind but not applying them in my life. At some point, the truth has to move from our heads and be put into action. (James 1:22) We have to go from someone who knows the truth to someone who applies the truth. This is so important in your walk to freedom. You must not only learn God's word but also begin to put it into practice in your everyday life.

Let me give you an example. We all know that if we want to accumulate a nest egg for retirement we have to start saving while we are still young. We know if we place $100 a month in a savings account or mutual fund, over time that money will grow. Eventually the $100 a month will turn into thousands of dollars. We know this is true, but do we take action? Some people do, and thirty years later they have a sizeable fund to begin planning retirement. Others never apply this basic principle and are left wondering how they are going to get by in their senior years. Knowing they needed to put money in a savings account was not enough. The same is true in our spiritual lives. Knowing the truths of God's word, His promises, and instructions, are useless if we never apply them in our lives. We wind up spiritually bankrupt, wishing we had applied what we knew was true all along.

For so long I knew what to do but never did it. You may feel the same way. Most of us, for whatever reason, often stop short of applying God's word in our lives. We live imprisoned because we never take action. We live in bondage and wonder why God will not change us. I hope you will not only seek to understand these basic truths, but I hope you begin to apply them. Otherwise, you are reading this book in vain.

This chapter contains some basic information about some of the most powerful truths from the Bible. These are the same principles that have encouraged and empowered Christians since Paul and Peter themselves taught these same truths two thousand years ago.

God is love. (1 John 4:15-16) This is a fact we must accept and trust in if we hope to live in freedom. God loves us despite our mistakes and sinfulness. God loves us regardless of our failures and inner darkness. We cannot earn God's love, but we can refuse to accept it.

Many Christians know God sent Jesus to die for their sins and will tell others "For God so loved the world, that He gave His only begotten Son, that whoever believes in Him shall not perish, but have eternal life." (John 3:16) Yet those same Christians may feel like God hates them, is mad at them, or has turned His back on them. There are so many different reasons why we might feel these ways, but the truth is these are all lies.

God loves us. He does not reject us when we fail. Instead, He is waiting, longing for us to seek Him and ask for forgiveness and help. (Luke 15:11-32) This is a fact we must embrace. It is a vital part of the transformation process. It is a step towards freedom.

If you are someone who has trouble believing God loves you, I encourage you to research scripture and write down every verse you can find that tells you God loves you unconditionally. Make a habit of looking over these verses daily. Read a few every day, memorize as many as you can, and let the truth set you free.

The lie is God will turn His back on you or that He has given up on you. The truth is God loves you.

God truly wants us to be free. (John 8:34-36) Sin is slavery. Jesus knows this. When we submit to sin, we are mastered and controlled by it. (Romans 6:16) This is slavery. This is prison. If we never break free we will remain tormented, trapped, and hopeless. If we remain in sin we will never live in the freedom God wants to give us.

Jesus died to set us free from sin and death. (Romans 6:8-18) When we understand God sincerely wants us to be able to live outside the prison walls, we can see Him in a different light. God doesn't want us to break free from sin because He wants to keep us from having fun. Instead He knows everytime we sin we are being drawn deeper into darkness. The chains become tighter and our joy is stolen from us. Sin leads to death. (Romans 6:23, James 1:15) Not just physical death, but the death of marriages, families, jobs, ministries, dreams, and every other thing that fills our lives with joy and meaning. God wants to keep us from suffering needlessly. He wants to bless us, but sin prevents that from happening.

We are often told by our society that doing sinful things makes us happier. We are told freedom is in doing whatever we want whenever we want. We are told living God's way is no fun and boring. But the truth will set you free. I have lived in sin, and I have felt the chains clamp tight around my wrists and ankles. I have heard the cell door slam shut and tried to press it open. I have been enslaved, and it is not worth the few minutes of pleasure that sin brings. Giving into lust only made life miserable in the long run. It simply was not worth it.

God wants to set us free. He truly wants what is best for us. God is willing to hurt our feelings and confront our sin because He knows it is holding us captive. God loves us enough to tell us the truth.

God loves you enough, and cares about you enough, and wants to set you free so badly that He not only sent Jesus to die for your sins but allows His Holy Spirit to indwell your sinful body. God is willing to place His holiness within you to help you overcome. This is an amazing truth. This is the same Holy Spirit that empowered Peter, James, and Paul. This is the same Holy Spirit that has guided Billy

Graham and Beth Moore. By His Holy Spirit God will empower and guide you to real freedom. I hope you can grasp this truth.

The lie is God's ways are binding and boring, a prison of rules and regulations. The truth is God's way will give you true joy and life, real freedom.

God wants to set us free and has given us very real and basic instructions to follow. (Psalm 119:9-16) This is so important. For example, the Bible is very clear on sexual purity. First Thessalonians 4:1-8 cannot be mistaken if we are looking for the truth. God clearly commands us to learn to control our sexual urges. God clearly teaches us to abstain from any form of sexual immorality.

He has not hidden His will. He has not covered up the facts. He has not left His commands in the shadows. God has plainly told us what He expects. God has publicly declared what choices He blesses and which ones He opposes. God has very boldly given us instructions to follow. The problem is these often conflict with our human nature. The truth is we do not like His instructions so we rely on our own desires and the ideals of this world. We look for other answers because we do not like His answers.

I promise you, whatever struggle you are dealing with, God has given you a clear instruction about it. You may not know the Bible well, but you probably have at least read or heard one verse that tells you how God feels about your struggle. The question then becomes: will you listen to His word and apply it to your life? Or will you try to justify your actions? Will you listen to an "expert" or a friend who tells you its okay to keep doing what you already know is wrong in God's eyes?

If your struggle is anger, God has given you an answer. If it is lust, you know how God feels. If it is greed, the Bible is clear about the love of money. If it is an addiction to prescription painkillers, you already know the answer. Will you apply the truth? Will you become a "doer" of the word? (James 1:22-25)

The lie is God's will is hard to understand. The truth is God has made it clear, through His word, what He wants us to do and how it will bless us.

God will help you, but you must obey and follow Him to find true freedom. (Hebrews 13:1-6) God didn't leave us as orphans to fend for ourselves. Yet the truth is we too, must flee from evil. We must take steps towards freedom. For example, I must limit my exposure to TV programs and movies I know contain questionable material. To allow myself to be exposed to sexual images and content is foolish. If I hope to walk in purity, I must walk on the path of purity. I cannot hope to walk down a path of sexual temptation regularly and ask God to simply take away my urges. That is basically "testing" God. It is foolish and dangerous. It is a guaranteed formula for failure.

Yes, I can lean on His strength and power. Yes, I can call upon His name and claim His promises. Yes, I can ask for help in my time of need. These are all true, but am I doing what I need to do? Am I personally engaged in the battle for my freedom?

I have learned I must do my part. God will draw closer to me, and help me but I cannot ignore my responsibilities. Just as salvation comes through believing and confessing, freedom comes through trusting in God and living in obedience. This is not easy, but it is essential. Please do not overlook this part of breaking free.

The lie is we have to do all the work ourselves. The truth is God is at work within us and around us, but we must do our part as well.

God blesses those who seek Him. (Psalm 119:1-2) There is an obvious truth that rings true throughout scripture. God blesses those who obey and seek Him. (Malachi 3:8-12, Hebrews 11:6) God's special favor and blessings are not poured out on everyone. He has the right and authority to give as He wills and He has set some conditions upon blessing His people. This may not be a popular view of scripture, but it is true!

Also, Luke 18:28-30 shows us God's blessings and rewards are not just heavenly. Yes, we can expect to receive rewards in heaven according to the promises of God, but He also blesses us in this present age. When we submit to His will, obey His commands, and trust in His promises, we will be blessed.

I want to make something very plain here. We do not "earn" God's blessings, but He has set conditions upon His blessings. He is God and has made it clear that He cannot bless us if we walk in disobedience. If we choose to ignore His commands and live as we please, He, as a just and loving God, cannot reward us and bless us. It would contradict who He is as God. A holy God cannot bless and reward un-holiness! (God can use un-holiness but that is a different thing altogether. We will look at this in more detail later.)

I hope you can see the significance of this truth. When we walk in obedience, God can pour out His blessings upon us. He has promised to take care of our needs if we will seek His Kingdom. (Matthew 6:33) I am not trying to teach that if we obey all His commands nothing bad will ever happen in our lives. I am not trying to say God is a "heavenly genie" who will grant all of our requests if we can somehow jump through the right hoops in life. But the fact remains the Bible clearly teaches that God pours His favor out on those who live as He commands. This is truth and can change your life if you will grab hold of the implications. If you want to live under the favor and blessings of God, it will require submitting to His will and not your own.

The lie is what we do after we are saved really does not matter to God or make much difference in life or in heaven. The truth is God blesses those who obey and seek Him.

God can and will redeem my mistakes and turn evil into good. (Genesis 50:20) God is a redeemer. He is able to take evil and use it for good. God is able to take our mistakes and use them to teach us. He is able to use our errors, our struggles, and our failures, and make something amazing happen.

It is the very thing that nearly destroyed my life that has given me a new passion and zeal for life. It is my struggle that drives me to seek God and to share His word with others. It is the realization of what He has saved me from that draws me closer to Him. It is my personal understanding of sin and His grace that compel me to share the gospel with others.

Paul writes about a "thorn in the flesh." (2 Corinthians 12:7-10) He pleaded with God to end his struggle. Yet the Lord showed him it was his struggle that made him rely on God. It had become a useful thing in God's hands. Paul would not have been the great man of God he was had it not been for the "thorn."

So, too, God has used my struggle to shape me, to teach me, and to help me see how much I need Him. He has used it to humble me and give me a heart of compassion. He has also used my struggle to help me teach about His love and mercy. God is indeed a great redeemer. He wants to not only set you free from the prison you are in, but He also wants to redeem your struggle and use it for good.

I hope you can see that redeeming evil is not the same as blessing evil. God can take our poor choices and rebellion and use them to change us, get our attention, or whatever He chooses to do. He is almighty and sovereign. We can trust Him to hold us accountable but at the same time redeem our poor choices. Doing so brings glory and honor to His name by revealing His sovereignty, power, and goodness.

The lie is once you have messed up, you are disqualified from serving God in a powerful way. The truth is God most often uses our biggest mistakes for His glory.

These are the kinds of eye opening, life-changing truths that can set you free. These are the kinds of verses and passages God can use to loosen the chains in your life. Only two things must happen. You need to grow in your knowledge of the Bible, and you need to apply what you learn to your life. To know is not enough. You must begin to take steps of faith.

You can be free. God is ready and willing to work in and with you. Are you really ready to do whatever it takes? Are you really ready to do whatever He asks? Are you really ready to apply His truth in your life? You cannot find freedom any other way. He has a plan. He has a way out, but you have to be willing to take it.

The rest of this book focuses in on these basic truths in various ways. Through Bible verses, personal examples, and practical application tips I hope this book will help you overcome your struggle. The basic truths I have outlined above are real and life-changing. The key to success is in moving from "knowing these things" to applying them in our everyday lives.

Before you move on, I hope you will examine your heart and determine where you stand with the Bible. Do you believe it is literally the inspired word of God and is the supreme standard and authority? Do you judge the Bible by other books and ideals, or do you instead judge everything else by God's word? Your answer to this question will reveal a lot about your faith as a Christian. Simply put, if you don't consider the Bible as the inspired word of God and as the ultimate authority, then you will probably never fully give yourself to seeking it, nor will you base your life on its promises, commands, and insights. Basically, you will never apply what you "know" if you really don't believe in its power and authority. This is a question you need to sincerely address.

Bring Your Struggle into the Light

J esus came to give us hope. Jesus came to bring us into a relationship with God. (Luke 1:77-79) He wants to shine His light of hope and peace into our lives. By doing this He can expose our areas of weakness, our personal struggles, and help us find the paths to freedom. Jesus died to set you free and will show you the way. It is then up to you to follow the path to freedom, peace, and joy.

John 1:5 reminds us that we are by nature opposed to the light of truth. We live in darkness and like it. We are sinful creatures and often flee from the light because it exposes our sin. (John 3:19) We fear the truth because we understand that in the light we can no longer hide. We are confronted by the brightness of truth and often flee back into the dark prison cell.

It is so easy to become "comfortable" within the walls of our prisons. We often settle in and begin to think we are okay, free, and full of life. When the light exposes the truth and we see the bars, the cold damp floor, and the windowless walls, we pull back. The light exposes our condition, and we do not like it at all. But instead of crying out to the source of light and asking for a way out, we tend to withdraw, pulling away into a dark corner, hoping the light will leave so we can feel comfortable again.

Unfortunately, I know this first hand. For so long I didn't want God to expose my secret because I knew I would have to change. I wanted to remain in the darkness. I found pleasure and excitement there. Yet somehow I knew it was opposed to all that was good, and it was destroying my life. No matter how I tried to reason it away or to justify my actions, I knew it was wrong and harmful. There was enough light within me to show me the truth. The Holy Spirit was at work.

As God revealed more and more of His word and truth to me, I began to see more and more clearly that I was in a prison of selfishness, lust, and immorality. I began to realize I was not free to sin but trapped by sin. I began to desire freedom.

As the light of God shone into my soul I could see the darkness. I could also begin to envision the hope of victory. I started to believe I could escape the prison of pornography. The light of truth was illuminating the path of peace, and I wanted to take it, I wanted out of the prison cell that once held me captive.

The key was taking steps of faith into the light. It was painful. Confession is always painful at first. But as a shot brings medicine into contact with a virus or bacteria so confession brings the light into contact with darkness. Healing begins, hope blossoms, and peace begins to take the place of despair.

Once I was able to fully confess my sinfulness to God, He was able to begin to deal with my problem. The more I exposed the darkness within me to the light of God, the more I began to see I was on the path of healing and forgiveness. I began to desire purity and obedience. I began to truly desire to live a life that would be pleasing to God.

If you hope to be free you must let the light of God expose the struggle within. His word will shine deep within your soul and reveal the secrets hidden there. The Holy Spirit will whisper rays of light into your life and help you see what is holding you deep within the prison walls. You will see the chains. You will know the truth, and the truth will set you free.

Once you are able to see clearly that you have a struggle which is holding you captive, you can then bring it fully into the light. This is not easy. It is not a one time event. It is a process that truly never ends. As you hold your struggle into the light you will not like what you see. It will frighten you and surprise you. You may even want to withdraw again into the darkness. It may take you several attempts, but finally you will be able to fully expose your sinfulness. You will be able to fully confess who you are before your God. You will feel the pain of regret and sorrow, but it will be replaced by joy and peace as the warm light comforts you. You will once again believe you can overcome. You will once again dream of freedom.

If you truly want to break free and run into the peace of God, you are going to have to expose the lies, sin, and darkness within. There is no other way. You may know the truth already but just cannot express it before God. You may not want to say it out loud because the words are too hurtful and dark, but confession is the key to allowing the light of God to shine on your struggle.

We must know who we are, and we must be able to admit our sinfulness. Only then will God fully expose the darkness. Only then will we be able to receive His healing ointment. Only then will we see the darkness for what it is and then will we see the gate swing open wide and hear the chains fall to the floor. You may already know this is true, but you must apply it if it is going to change your life.

The light of God's word brings about new insight and wisdom. God will open your eyes to new and powerful truths. Once you begin to have these types of revelations you can apply them in your life. Then you will begin to see a transformation in your actions and desires. You will find that you are walking in freedom.

To Walk In Freedom You Need a Lamp

O nce you have been able to allow God to shine the truth into your life, you will have to begin taking steps along the path of freedom. You are going to have to make some choices which will enable you to move further and further away from the prison that has held you captive.

God has given us some pretty clear instructions within His word, and we must choose to live by His word if we hope to remain free. This is not easy because it requires discipline and patience and even some suffering. It takes time to live in freedom. We must learn to adjust and adapt.

One of the most important things I have done is to find scriptures that give me wisdom and insight. God has filled the Bible with advice, warnings, and promises. I have learned to seek these out. I have written down, memorized, and prayed over passages and verses that help me see clearly. They shine His light upon my path, expose pitfalls, and warn me of upcoming danger. His word is truly a "lamp unto my feet." (Psalm 119:105)

We each need our own "lamp." Everyone of us is at a different place, on a different walk, and at a different level of spiritual maturity. What helps me may not help you. What opens my eyes and gives me light may not impact anyone else. There is no single scripture, or passage, or truth that touches everyone. How many times have you heard someone quote a scripture that changed his life and you are completely unimpressed? They are moved or empowered, but the same words do nothing for you.

My point is this: God has given us enough biblical text and variety that we can each find our own lamp. It has to be personal. Your lamp has to open up *your* eyes and shine light upon *your* path for *your* feet to follow. It has to connect with *your* soul. The Holy Spirit has to reveal to each person the truths that will impact that individual. We cannot force this but instead must wait for God to speak to our hearts as we seek Him.

How much frustration and disappointment could be avoided if every person could find their own lamp? Instead, most of us try to use someone else's. We hear how a verse or passage or spiritual discipline impacted someone and so we try to take his lamp and attempt to walk down our dark path. Before long we realize we are still in darkness, and are confused and hopeless. Then we begin to doubt the power of God's word and draw back into our cell. The problem is we try to use the word that God spoke to someone else instead of listening to the words He is speaking to us.

God has a lamp for you. It has to be yours. It also must be constantly filled with new oil. This is accomplished by constantly seeking the Lord in His word, in prayer, and in worship. Again, there is no magic formula. What I do, how God connects with me, even varies as my life changes. There are times I feel so drawn to Him in prayer. Other times I cannot seem to study His word enough. Still other times just being outside on a moonless night fills my soul with joy, awe, and peace.

But one thing I have learned is that my lamp will run out of oil if I do not invest time and effort into filling it regularly. In other words, you must make a purposeful choice to find ways to connect with God. It may be through music and time alone in the morning. It may be by sitting quietly with God for a half hour in the afternoon. It may be by joining a Bible study group. It may even be a combination of these. The idea is seek God. Bring your lamp to Him so He can fill it with oil.

As you grow and learn and your lamp is filled with new oil you will begin to experience new freedoms in Christ. You will begin to see things in a different light so to speak. You will start to recognize there are things in your life that need to change. You will come to understand God has been with you the whole time, drawing you to Him. You will also find you want to do things that are pleasing to God just because of who He is and what He has already done.

What I have discovered is that I am slowly changing. My mind is being transformed. (Romans 12:1-2) God's word, the Holy Spirit, and prayer are changing me. My interests have changed. My desires have changed. My ideals have changed. They are beginning to line up with those I read about in the Bible.

I have a new passion to do what is pleasing to God. He has shown me that no pleasure is worth it if it is not pleasing to Him. No financial gain is worth it if I have to receive it in any way that opposes His commands. No honor or reward is worth it if I have to compromise what I know to be true from God's word. No thrill, no rush, nothing is worth it if I have to gain it by acting in a way that places me in opposition to God's revealed truths.

This has been empowering. I can avoid confusion and face temptations head on. What does the Bible say? Is lust of any form a sin? Yes, so I must avoid anything that would cause me to lust. Is sordid gain wrong? Yes, so I must make sure I am not taking advantage of anyone. Is drunkenness a sin? Yes, so I must not become intoxicated in any way. The answers are there, so what will my response be? Will I act on what I know to be true? Will I obey God's word, my lamp, or will I seek the advice of another, one who will tell me what I want to hear instead of what I need to hear? Will I set down my lamp and seek a different light when I don't like what the truth reveals?

The truth is there, but I have to act on it. This is not always easy because I sometimes have to surrender my will to follow His. I don't always like doing things His way, but I can see now it's the only way to remain free. I am learning that choosing to obey God always produces the best results, not always the easiest, but certainly always the best. When I let the truth illuminate my path, it helps me to take the right steps.

The same thing will work for you. The more you fill your soul with the wisdom, warnings, and promises of God, the more you will be empowered. Your lamp will shine brighter and give you a better view. It is really amazing.

God wants to help us see clearly. He truly does want us to make good choices. He really does care.

Do you have a lamp? How is God shining His light upon your path? The resources are there, are you using them? He has provided various ways for you to fill your lamp with oil, are you taking advantages of those opportunities? I hope you will purposely go to God through various means and let Him constantly provide you with oil.

Thorns in the flesh

God uses our struggles to get our attention. (2 Corinthians 12:7-10) God knows our places of birth, our circumstances of life, and will use our struggles to draw us to Him. (Acts 17:26-27) Our struggles can become the very things that point us to God. Our weaknesses allow us to see His glory, goodness, compassion, love, mercy, authority, and power. They also allow us to see our sinful nature. Our struggles in a sense lead us to God.

I am not suggesting that God is pleased with sin or that He desires for us to remain in our struggle. Yet He is the God who uses evil for good. (Genesis 50:20, Deuteronomy 23:5) He will turn our weaknesses into blessings so to speak. We have to come to that place where we see our need of Him, our need to be forgiven, and our need to give our lives to Christ; if we never understand we are sinful, we will never ask for forgiveness. Our individual struggles help us see we are just like the rest of mankind, sinful and in need of a Savior.

Instead of letting the enemy hold us back and keep us in the chains of our struggles we can call upon our Creator and allow Him to set us free. When we receive His love, grace, and mercy we will glorify Him and worship Him in Spirit and in Truth.

My struggle with pornography constantly reminds me that God has set me free, forgiven me, and redeemed my past. I am left in awe and wonder and admiration of His kindness and love. I cannot help but glorify Him because I know what He has saved me from. I know the depths of His forgiveness and grace. I also know the joy of receiving mercy when it was the last thing I deserved.

I also know that I am no different from the man who is in prison for rape. I know I am no different from the man who sits behind his computer, trapped in sin, while his family falls apart around him. I am no different from the drug addict who will lie and steal for his next high. My struggle has revealed my need of a Savior. My struggle has shown me that without Jesus I am hopeless and powerless.

Do you know you are a sinner? Has God used your struggle to expose your sinful nature? Do you know you need His forgiveness and strength and hope? Has your struggle brought you to the point in your life when you realize you need Jesus?

Though I am not proud of my past I can see it has led me to the cross and to forgiveness. It has shown me I am far from perfect and in need of salvation. It has revealed God's love and mercy to my broken heart. God has used my addiction to pornography to change me and draw me to Him.

I never want to go back, no more than I want to go back to wearing diapers and drinking from a bottle.

Yet I can sincerely say my struggle was a growing and somewhat necessary part of my life. Apart from seeing my sin and darkness through my addiction, I do not know if I would have given my life to Jesus.

Think for a minute about the "Rich Young Ruler" as mentioned in Matthew 19:16-22. This man of wealth and good works could not see his sinfulness. He was seeking eternal life but had a struggle; he loved money. Jesus shined the Light of truth upon this man's dependency on wealth, but the young ruler left in sorrow. He was not willing to see the truth when Jesus revealed it so He remained in darkness.

It seems this young man was by human standards good and was doing all the right things. He had not murdered anyone. He was not a habitual liar and had not committed adultery; he was a good guy. He apparently was also spiritual, after all the man was seeking God and faithfully followed the Jewish traditions. By most people's standards this guy had it made. Yet he was in a prison. The young man knew something was missing. There was a longing in his heart for eternal life.

Jesus gave him the opportunity to break free. The Lord shined His lamp upon greed and the love of money. He brought the young man to a point of crisis. Would he continue to hold onto his possessions or would he grab hold of the Savior? Would he admit he loved the things of the world and confess it to Jesus? Would he proclaim his name was "greed?" Or would he remain bound in chains?

Jesus didn't force the man to let go. He didn't pry the money and possessions from his hands. Instead

He gave him an option, a choice; walk free or remain enslaved; choose life or death. In the same way God uses our struggles to offer us life. We are each given the opportunity to let go of the darkness so we can embrace life. Our struggle actually reveals the contrast. It exposes our sinfulness and allows us to see there is a better alternative.

I wonder, what would have happened in the young man's life had he confessed his sin and followed Jesus? Would God have redeemed his past and used him to touch other people's lives? Is it possible God would have used his skills and reputation to bless many more people? Who knows what might have happened had he not turned away.

One of the most amazing truths of God's word is this: our past doesn't disqualify us from God's love or usefulness within His Kingdom. Instead our past qualifies us for mercy and the ability to share His love with others. I hope you can see this life-changing truth. Yes, living in sin keeps you from being a "vessel of honor" and hinders the work of God in and around you. However, turning from sin and receiving His grace cleanses you and makes you a vessel that is useful to the Master. How we respond to His offer of forgiveness and restoration makes all the difference.

What is your story? Can you proclaim God's grace and mercy? Has your struggle been exposed? Has God redeemed your struggle and turned it into a blessing? Will you take the hand of God and begin to rejoice in His grace?

Receive Forgiveness

O—

One of the hardest things to do when it comes to walking away from an addiction or habitual sin is to receive forgiveness. I hated myself for so long. I knew I was disrespecting Val and jeopardizing our marriage. I knew I was offending God and I knew I was harming my family and risking everything for a few cheap thrills. This brought a great amount of shame and guilt into my life.

I knew I was a Christian and that God had forgiven me of my sins, but I also knew I was not living in a way that was pleasing to Him. Looking back, I can see this caused me to stay away from church, Bible study, and even Christian relationships because I felt guilty and dirty. To top it all off, I still really didn't want to let go of my habit. Even though I knew it was wrong and harmful, I enjoyed it. This brought even more guilt and shame into my life. The cycle continued for so long.

It is hard to say you are sorry, but it is even harder to receive undeserved grace. We know we need to be forgiven but feel so unworthy to receive forgiveness. You know what? That is the point! If you were worthy, you would not need forgiveness in the first place!

The Bible tells us Jesus came to die for us while we were still sinners. (Luke 5:32, Romans 5:8) This confirms the truth that we can receive forgiveness when we don't deserve it. This is so difficult but so important. We don't deserve to be forgiven; that is what makes His grace so amazing!

We are raised to earn our place in society, in school, and even in church sometimes. So we try so hard to earn God's love or we struggle to pay Him back. We want to somehow earn forgiveness. Of course this is a debt we can never repay. Yet we try, only to fall short once again. Instead of earning our way out, we actually become more and more indebted to Him.

The simple truth is Jesus has already paid the price in full. (Hebrews 10:10) We cannot repay Him because we can do nothing to redeem ourselves. Besides, God never asks us to repay Him but rather to live for Him as a result of His mercy. We can only do that by receiving His grace and then allowing Him to heal us. As we walk with God we are transformed and changed. That is truly what He desires: people who are transformed into the likeness of Christ.

Before you can move on and walk in freedom, you must accept the forgiveness that God offers you. If you are not already a Christian, you can turn to God and through faith in Jesus Christ, receive forgiveness and eternal life. (John 3:16, Romans 10:9-13, Ephesians 2:8-9) If you are a Christian then you need to confess your sins, repent, and ask for forgiveness. (1 John 1:9) He will forgive you. He will restore you. He will heal you, but you must acknowledge your sin and seek His forgiveness.

I love the words Jesus spoke to Peter the night before He was betrayed. (John 13:5-10) Jesus wraps Himself with a towel and begins to wash the feet of the disciples. Peter, in his normally brash style, rebukes the Lord. Peter just couldn't accept the grace Jesus offered him. He was taken aback, how could the Messiah wash his feet? Yet Jesus used Peter's stubbornness to teach him, and us, a valuable lesson.

Jesus confronts Peter's attitude and reminds him He is the one with the authority. Peter then does a 180 degree turn. He wants to obey Christ and so asked to be completely washed from head to toe. Yet in verse ten Jesus points out that these men have already been bathed and are clean. He is referring to the fact that the disciples had washed thoroughly in preparation for the Passover meal. Yet Jesus points out that their feet are dirty. As they had walked along the paths and roads after bathing, their feet became contaminated; the dust, dung, and other filth along the roadways and paths had clung to their sandaled feet. Though their bodies were "clean," their feet needed to be washed.

As Jesus often did, He was using things within the physical realm to teach about spiritual truths. In this case, Jesus was pointing out that though they believed He was the Messiah, had been baptized, and had left their homes to follow Him, they still needed an occasional washing. In other words, they had repented, confessed Jesus as Lord, and were baptized as a symbol of their "dying to sin." Therefore, they were clean spiritually but like us, continued to make some sinful choices. Since they had already committed to following Jesus, they were technically clean. Yet they needed the fresh filth to be washed away. Jesus then freely offered to wash their dirty feet.

This is a picture of confessing the sins we commit after we are "born again" so we can receive the forgiveness God freely offers us. (1 John 1:8-2:2) We need this, even though we are saved, because we still commit sins after salvation.

The point I believe Jesus made is this: once you have received Christ you are forgiven and you no longer need to be "washed completely again." Yet as we live in this world we will make mistakes. Our feet will get dirty, so to speak, with the filth of poor choices and we will need the Master to "wash our feet."

(He then goes on to command us to do the same for others. We are told in the Bible to forgive as we have been forgiven. This includes forgiving people who have already asked for forgiveness in the past. God's grace is limitless and we should never withhold mercy when we deal with those who offend us. (Matthew 18:21-35) God never withholds His mercy from those who seek His forgiveness so we should never stop forgiving those who hurt us.)

Christians, when we find ourselves in sin we need to confess those sins and let Jesus wash our feet. You are saved and have no need to be completely washed again but you do need His love and forgiveness, receive it as Peter did. Let Jesus wash away the sins that have caked your feet as you've walk through this life.

Some people become confused about having to ask for forgiveness after they have been born again. The Bible tells us Jesus died for all of our sins and they have been washed away. (Ephesians 1:5-7, Revelation 1:5) This occurs at the time of salvation according to John 3:16 and Romans 10:9-10. These scriptures tell us that when we acknowledge Jesus as the Savior, then confess our sinfulness and ask to be forgiven, we are saved and given eternal life. We are born again and sealed by the Holy Spirit. (John 3:1-8, Ephesians 1:13-14) This is the basis of our faith. This is the truth of the gospel. This is our only hope of salvation.

If you are a Christian then you understand your need of a Savior and have already asked to be forgiven. So why then do you need to ask to be forgiven again? This is where we can become confused.

The fact is that after we are saved we still continue to make bad choices. Even though we have been adopted and sealed as a child of God we are still sinners because we continue to have a sinful nature within us. After salvation we are not automatically perfect and will sin against God again, no matter how hard we try not to. These sins then have to be dealt with.

The good news is that once we have found redemption and have been given eternal life we are secure in Christ. (1 Peter 1:3-9) We are "kept" or protected by God and are covered by His amazing grace. The Bible assures us we are not in any way saved by our works. (Romans 11:6, Ephesians 2:1-10) Salvation does not come by being a good person or by avoiding sin. Salvation is a gift from God that can only be obtained by faith in Jesus Christ. (John 14:6)

Yet our sins after salvation still affect us. (Romans 6:12-16, James 4:1-4) Sin hinders the Spirit of God within us and affects our spiritual maturity. Sin destroys relationships and causes pain in our lives. Also, we will give an accounting of our life one day, as a child of God. (Romans 14:10-12, 2 Corinthians 5:10) Our life and faithfulness as a Christian will somehow affect us on that day. 1 Corinthians 3:10-15 make it pretty clear that our life as Christians matters to God, not for salvation, because that has already been secured, but in other significant ways.

When we realize we have sinned we need to ask for forgiveness. God is gracious and quick to wash our feet when His we cry out in repentance and ask for mercy. (Psalm 86:5, 1 John 1:9) Because He is a gracious and merciful God, He will forgive us when we acknowledge our sin and ask to be purified. Remember you cannot earn forgiveness, you can only receive it.

You may think you are beyond His love and forgiveness. You may think you have made so many mistakes that God has given up on you. I assure you this is not true. In fact the Bible teaches us that God's grace actually increases when the amount of sin increases. (Romans 5:20) The Bible also teaches us that those who have been forgiven the most understand God's grace the most. (Luke 7:36-50) If you have sinned greatly, God's grace is much greater. If you will receive His forgiveness then you will know the value of His mercy. You will know what it is like to be touched by His grace.

Another important part of God's grace is the fact that Jesus understands your temptations. The Bible tells us that He was tempted in every way that we are. (Hebrews 4:15) He knows what it feels like to have a tempting thought pop into His head. He knows what its like to crave something you cannot have. Jesus understands because He has been there. He is compassionate and sympathetic because He has walked in your shoes. Jesus understands what its like to be human.

God does not hate us and does not become disgusted with us when we fail. Instead, His heart breaks and yearns to bring healing into our lives. He knows we are sinful. He knows we have a human nature. (Psalm 78:38-39) He is a compassionate God who is slow to anger. In fact the only way to miss out on God's grace is by not receiving it!

Hosea 14:1-7 teaches us God longs to forgive and restore us. If we will return to Him and seek His forgiveness, He will have compassion on His people. He will heal us and love us freely. If we will receive what He is offering and seek to remain faithful, He will prosper us and turn our shame into His glory. He will redeem our mistakes and use us to testify of His great love and forgiveness. (Psalm 51:5-13)

His love and mercy and healing are waiting on you. God offers you grace. It is free. The forgiveness you need and desire is available, but you must receive it.

It is a Spirit Thing

S omething you have to realize about your struggle is you cannot gain control simply by trying harder. Most people have a limited amount of willpower and are seldom ever able to overcome deep-seeded habits. Very few people are able to stop looking at pornography, walk away from drugs, or drop other addictions "cold turkey." The majority of us try but fail, try but fail again, and finally give up when it comes to fighting to overcome our addictions and struggles.

Right after I surrendered to the ministry a couple of wise Christians were able to help me see overcoming my struggle required more than willpower. I had to rely on spiritual help. I had to lean on a power that is greater than me. I am, of course, referring to the Holy Spirit.

The Bible teaches us that if we will focus on the Spirit we can overcome the flesh. In other words, if I will give myself to God's way of doing things, I can overcome sin. Sin is a spiritual issue; therefore, overcoming sin is a spiritual battle. (Galatians 5:16-17, Ephesians 6:12)

As long as we try to overcome our struggle by just trying harder, we will fail. We instead must focus our minds on the Spirit. Romans 8:5-9 shows us that minds set on the flesh will result in sin. On the other hand, minds set on the Spirit will result in victories. Minds set on our addictions and struggles will draw us deeper into temptation and despair, but minds set on God will help us make godly choices and discover hope.

Self-control is a portion of the fruit of the Spirit. (Galatians 5:22-23) This is a gift from God that enables us to make changes in our life that are beyond our natural ability. Once you are a Christian, God can fill you with the Holy Spirit and empower you beyond your human nature. He can impart His power directly to you. He can then produce all the amazing portions of the fruit of the Spirit in your life. Isn't that what He did through the Christians we read about in the Bible? They were not superhuman with unnatural abilities. They were men and women just like us who were empowered by the Spirit of God! (Acts 14:8-15, James 5:17-18)

So how do you enact the power of the Spirit in your life? The first step is to understand you have the Spirit within you, if you are a Believer. As I mentioned earlier, the Bible teaches us God seals every new Christian with the Holy Spirit. (1 Corinthians 6:19-20, 2 Corinthians 1:20-22, Ephesians 1:13-14) Have you come to terms with this truth? God the Holy Spirit dwells within you if you have received Jesus as Lord!

This is enough to make you sit back and think for awhile. God is living in you, identifying you as His child, communicating with you, guiding you, and empowering you. I hope this truth sinks deep into your soul.

Once you understand God indwells you, you can begin to experience His transforming power. The Bible tells us "all things are possible with God." (Matthew 19:26, Philippians 4:13) I hope you understand the significance of this revelation. If God is within you and empowering you then all things are possible. You can overcome! You can break free from the addictions and habits that have held you captive for so long.

How do you begin to experience His power? You can ask to be "filled with the Spirit." This is basically asking God to empower you. The Holy Spirit is the giver of gifts and the one who equips us with God's wisdom, discernment, and all He has to offer. It is the Spirit of God that bears the fruit of God within us. For instance James 1:5-8 encourages us to ask God for wisdom when we lack it. If we recognize our need for wisdom, then we should seek His wisdom by asking to be filled with His Spirit, since it is by the Holy Spirit that God imparts His gifts. Once you've asked God to give you wisdom, believe He has heard and responded to your request. Then expect to be wise and to make godly choices. By faith in His promise, trust He will give you wisdom and understanding beyond your own ability.

Do you realize this kind of power and wisdom is available to you? God has told us to ask to be filled.

We need to recognize the gifts that are available to us through His Holy Spirit just as we need to understand what we are missing when we fail to ask. This is so vital. How often do we miss out on freedom, power, peace, and self-control just because we fail to seek God's help and to rely on His promises?

By faith, ask God to fill you with His Holy Spirit. (Luke 11:13) God will sustain you and guide you from within. He will give you the insight and power you need. The Lord will instruct you and give you wisdom. You then must listen to the Spirit.

I am still learning to listen. God speaks to me in many different ways. I cannot fully express each way nor do I expect God to connect with us all the same. I am learning to be sensitive to the Holy Spirit as I mature in Christ. This takes time and the faith to continue. He doesn't always guide me in the ways I expect Him to, but He is faithful to lead me and give me a way to overcome. (1 Corinthians 10:13)

I don't know if God speaks to me more now, or if I just listen better. I do "hear" Him more often, but I doubt it is because He is speaking more frequently or more directly to me. I believe I've just learned to listen more intently and with the expectation He will guide me. I hope you will learn to listen too.

When you are able to discern that God has revealed something to you then you must act upon the prompting of the Spirit. We can call this obeying, following, or responding to the Spirit. Basically it is a heartfelt knowledge that God has revealed something to you, and that you need to act upon that revelation. It may be a fresh revelation or an affirmation to a previously know truth. Either way, once you sense God has spoken you need to act in obedience. This is how God works within us and through us. The more we listen and the quicker we respond in obedience, the more we experience the power of God in and around us.

I have seen this work in various ways. For example, when I have had to deal with controversy and division in the church I have prayed and asked God to guide me. I will then try to spend time reading the Bible or Christian books based on leadership, or other relevant issues. Sure enough something will "pop out" from scripture or the book I am reading. It will be an answer to my prayer. I then have some choices to make. Will I believe this is God guiding me and will I apply it to the situation, even if I don't like the possible outcome? If I truly believe God has opened my eyes and given me instruction, I would be a fool to ignore it, even if it meant apologizing, taking a firm stand, or reversing my previously held position.

This is the way it usually happens for me. There are other times when I am inspired by a word or phrase. A lot of my sermons have come from a single word that suddenly grabs my attention or that keeps showing up in my study time.

Another example is when I sincerely pray God will help me reach out to those who need to be ministered to. Hours or even a few days later, I may have a sudden urge to go somewhere or talk to someone. I cannot remember all of the times I have "heard" God direct me in this way.

God will guide you past temptations and stumbling blocks. But you have to learn to trust the Holy Spirit is at work within you. He will help you make wise choices. If you truly want God to direct you, then you must learn to ask, seek, and listen. The Holy Spirit will guide you, but you must be actively involved in the process too.

Finally, you must do your best to avoid quenching the Spirit. The Bible teaches us we can act in a way that hinders or quenches or grieves the Spirit. (Ephesians 4:30, 1 Thessalonians 5:19) In other words, we can do things that obstruct the work of God within us. Sin offends and impedes the Holy Spirit. A lack of faith, a hard heart, rebellion, fear, and pride are examples of things that can prevent us from hearing the Spirit or keep us from responding to the Spirit.

I am learning to avoid those things that keep me from hearing God's voice. I desire to keep away from anything that prevents me from obeying God. This is not always easy, and I certainly find myself slipping at times. It is at that point, when the Spirit convicts me, that I need to repent, ask for forgiveness, and respond promptly. Can you see how this works?

I hope you understand the significance of the indwelling of the Holy Spirit. Apart from the power of God within us we would be powerless and hopeless. I encourage you to learn to tap into the power of God. Read more scripture about the promises God has given us about the Holy Spirit. This should help you increase your faith and your desire to ask to be filled and empowered. Remember, sin is a spiritual issue and is therefore a Spiritual battle, but you don't have to fight alone.

Accountability

W e not only have the Holy Spirit within us to help us, but God has given us another line of defense in our battle against sin. One of the most important elements of overcoming any addiction or sinful habit is accountability. Val was truly a Godsend in this area. She has allowed me to share my feelings, my secrets, my failures, and my victories. Her support and firm but loving refusal to accept my sinful habit, and her willingness to forgive me have been invaluable.

I have vowed to my wife not to lie to her, and I now take this promise very seriously. I have asked her to hold me accountable by directly asking me from time to time if I have slipped up. She also has the freedom to check my computer anytime she likes. I sincerely want to honor our marriage and obey God, but sometimes the flesh is weak. Knowing she is going to ask me point-blank and that she may pop in and look at my computer is just one more level of security.

We have learned to work together on this matter; she is my partner. Val has been wonderful in the recent years about not accusing me or jumping to conclusions. When I have faced temptation, she has learned to let me share my struggle without making me feel like a rat. Since we have developed a very open and honest relationship, we can both express how we feel, ask for support, pray for one another, and even admit our mistakes.

You may not be married or you may be like Val and me ten years ago. At that time we just didn't have the communication skills we needed as a couple. Either way, it is important that you find someone you can talk to, be honest with, and trust. This may be a parent, a sibling, a close friend, or a minister. Whoever it is, you need a person to hold you accountable and to give you the opportunity to express yourself openly.

God wants us to lean on one another. He has given us meaningful relationships to help us grow and overcome. (Ecclesiastes 4:9-12) Good friends, caring family members, and concerned brothers and sisters in Christ are essential in our walk with God and irreplaceable when it comes to breaking free from harmful habits.

Jesus Himself selected a small group of men that became His inner circle. Peter, James, and John were His closest friends and confidants. (Matthew 17:1, Mark 5:37, 14:33) These three men were important to Jesus. He had a special connection with them, and they met His need for companionship. These men were with Him during some of the most difficult moments of His life. They prayed for Him, talked to Him, and loved Him dearly.

We, too, need friends and family members we can share our hearts with. I have had good friends with whom I could confide, and I have had wonderful talks with my brothers about my struggle in the past couple of years. It has been a great help in my battle against pornography. It is truly amazing to me how many men understand where I am coming from. They can pray for me, give me advice, encourage me, and even get in my face if need be. (Proverbs 27:6) There may come a time when I need a friend or one of my brothers to be bold with me and to remind me of my desire to be free from all forms of lust. I truly would rather be confronted by someone I trust than to slip back into the dark prison.

It is also amazing how my sharing with friends and family members has blessed them too. God has used my willingness to seek accountability to help others with various struggles. When we reach out for help we often provide help. It is just one more example of God's redeeming power. God is amazing.

You need help. We all do. God designed us to function in community. We are called to gather in worship, to pray together, and to share our lives with other people. (Ephesians 5:19-21, Hebrews 10:25) If you want to break free and live outside of the prison walls, you are going to need help. You need a Christian community.

You also need one-on-one accountability. Your spouse, a parent, a family member you trust, a friend at work or church, or even a pastor can be a great accountability partner. It is so helpful to have someone you can open up with, and release your frustrations, and express your fears. This takes awhile and will not always come naturally. Yet it is worth your time and effort to invest yourself in solid, Christ-centered relationships.

You need someone who will hold you accountable. This person (or persons) needs to be honest, loving, and trustworthy. If you don't trust them, you will never be able to share your true feelings and struggles. They must also be the right kind of person. For instance, it wouldn't be wise for me to select a woman other than my wife to be my accountability partner. Obviously, that would be a huge mistake. Be wise; you certainly don't want to make things worse or to replace one sinful habit with another.

(You can ask your pastor or an elder at your local church to be involved in your effort to overcome your struggle, but be aware they may not be able to meet all of your expectations. They may be a helping hand, but are not able to meet everyone's needs all the time. If they are not able to be an accountability partner, perhaps they could point you to someone else who could help.)

Most of all, pray and ask God to place people in your life who can help you overcome. He will direct your path and open up relationships. It may take you awhile and you may be very surprised by those He brings into your life; so keep an open mind. God wants you to have close friends and family members who will give you wise counsel. Pray and trust Him to help you make those connections.

Don't Get Comfortable

One of the greatest dangers we face is becoming comfortable with sin. Instead of fleeing from immorality we often cozy up to it and pretend it's our friend. We justify, rationalize, and ignore it until we find ourselves consumed and imprisoned. We never intended for it to go that far but then feel powerless to break free. The prison door clangs shut behind us, and we sit wondering how it happened. Becoming comfortable with sin always causes harm.

A few chapters ago I mentioned pornography had become a sort of friend in my life. I was comfortable with it, even though I knew it was wrong and harmful. When we allow our sinful habits to settle in and become familiar to us, we are headed for heartache and pain. When we acclimate ourselves to sinful lifestyles, we are setting our futures up for disaster.

This was a common problem for people in the Bible too. God warned Israel about allowing sin to remain dangerously close. (Deuteronomy 7:1-6) He commanded them to wipe out all of those who worshipped false gods. The Lord knew the dangers that lay ahead of Israel if they married those who worshiped idols. God knew if they allowed the sin of idol worship to remain in the least bit they would eventually become casual about it and comfortable with those who practiced idolatry. The next step would be deadly as Israel would rebel against the Lord and go after false gods themselves.

King Solomon is said to be the wisest man that ever lived. Yet he had a struggle too. His problem is similar to mine. King Solomon had a sexual addiction. 1 Kings 11:1-8 describes the beginning of trouble for the king; Solomon loved foreign women. He was attracted to them and didn't obey the commandments of God. The Lord had warned Israel explicitly to avoid marrying foreign women because they worshiped false gods. Instead of fleeing from sin Solomon disobeyed God, married many foreign women, and then fell into idol worship himself.

Samson is perhaps the most famous Biblical example of becoming comfortable with sin. (Judges 16:4-27) God set Samson apart as a "judge" for Israel and gave him superhuman strength. He was supposed to abstain from immorality and devote himself to serving God but Samson had an eye for women; he had a real problem with lust.

Time after time the long-haired-strong-man would pick the wrong kind of women to hang around with. His first wife was a Philistine and nearly got him killed. (Judges 14 and 15) He was known to frequent prostitutes as well. (Judges 16:1-3) Finally he decided to settle down with another Philistine woman named Delilah.

Their relationship was rocky to begin with and Delilah kept trying to trick Samson into revealing his source of power. Instead of fleeing from her wicked schemes Samson played with fire. He teased her and tricked her but withheld the information, at least for a while. Samson was flirting with danger.

I have often wondered why Samson never left Delilah. According to the Bible she was pretty bold in her devious plot. Did Samson ever figure it out? Maybe he was only a jock and not much of a scholar? Either way, he had become comfortable with sin. He reclined in the arms of the enemy and was deceived. Once he disclosed his secret he was doomed. God warned him, but Samson refused to leave the ladies alone. He disobeyed, lived in sin, and opened himself up for a disastrous end.

When we get comfortable with sin, we do the same thing. It is foolish to think we can continue to live in a way that is in opposition to God's commands and never receive hurtful consequences. The Bible tells us "bad company corrupts good morals." (1 Corinthians 15:33) The fact is, when we get comfortable with sin, we bring harm upon ourselves, our loved ones, and our relationship with God.

Proverbs 22:24-25 give us another tidbit. If we associate with a person who is always negative or angry, we soon begin to take on their characteristics. The simple truth is that we begin to become like the people and environment we surround ourselves with.

When I was younger I used to hang out with different crowds. I could easily show up at church and fit right in. I could talk about the Bible, sing songs of worship, pray, and show everyone my "religious side." Later I might go to a friend's house and find myself cussing, drinking in excess, and telling off-color jokes. I would adapt to the crowd and circumstance. I could act as two completely different people. Chances are you know how this feels too.

It would be foolish to say that who the people we associate with and the environment we are in does not affect us. The simple fact is we are influenced by our surroundings. It is also true that the more comfortable we are around sin, the more likely we are to fall into sin.

For example, the first time a kid goes to a party where alcohol is being served, he may worry about being caught, refuse to have a beer, and feel nervous all night. However, the next time he goes out with his buddies, he is a little more relaxed and actually drinks a little. Weeks later he is the life of the party, and can't wait for the weekend to arrive, so he can live it up.

This scenario is true whether its alcohol, drugs, pornography, gossip, or gambling. The more we are exposed to sin, the more comfortable we become with it, and the more likely we are to fall into sin. Isn't that why we try to prevent our children from being surrounded by negative influences? We know children are affected by what they see, hear, and experience. We know if a child watches excessive violence on television or in video games, they are more likely to act aggressively. We know if a child is exposed to sexually explicit material, then they tend to become sexually active much younger than those who were not exposed to the graphic images. We know these things are true, and do our best to protect our children.

Does our propensity to be effected by our environment change as we get older? Perhaps somewhat, but we should never kid ourselves and deny the tendency we have to be influenced by our surroundings. We have seen the truth lived out time after time. Children, friends, loved ones, or even ourselves changed and influenced by sin, doing things we once swore we would never do. We have seen young celebrities surrounded by sinful influences only to be enslaved and destroyed soon after. Look at the preachers who have been publicly humiliated after succumbing to sin. The list goes on and on, teachers, lawyers, politicians, and policemen. No one is immune from the allure of sin.

The Bible warns us to be careful about who we associate with, where we go, and what we see and hear. These things impact our lives! The Bible also tells us to flee from sin. God knows our weaknesses, and wants us to run from those things that can draw us into darkness. If we fail to heed these warnings, we will find ourselves enslaved, wondering how we got there, wishing we had never taken that hit, typed in that address, or placed that first bet.

Perhaps we have all become a little too comfortable with sin? I have thought a lot about the changes in our society over the past three or four decades. As I reflect back on my childhood, and think about movies, television, and music, I realize that I have scen a major change in my lifetime. As a whole, we used to have a lower tolerance level for sexually explicit material. Slowly, our country has become comfortable with foul language, raunchy sit-coms, and over-the-top filth. It is everywhere, and few people really seem to care.

We have become accustom to the images, language, and lyrics. Yet we cannot seem to figure out why there are so many teen pregnancies, broken homes, rapes, and pedophiles. Is it possible that we have been exposed to so much for so long, that we really don't even notice it anymore? Have we just become too comfortable with it all?

There are so many areas that used to be black and white but are now gray. Do you ever wonder how these things are shaping us? Are there any areas in your life you would consider problems, places where sin has become the normal thing? You must be honest with yourself. Have you become comfortable with sin? If so, what are the possible outcomes?

Time

Over the past few years I have been able to look back on my life and really analyze my struggle and pick out areas of weakness and stumbling blocks. One of the big revelations for me has been how idle time played a major role in my struggle with pornography.

As I have reflected back on my life I can see boredom and extended times of idleness were major factors in my fight to break free. For example, when I was alone at home my mind would begin to focus on pornography. As my mind wandered, the temptation would grow. The longer I dwelt on my desires, the greater the urge to indulge would become. Before long I would act upon my thoughts and then sink back into regret and shame.

At the time I did not understand this cycle. Now as I have studied the Bible, I have found Biblical truths to encourage me and help me spend my time wisely. I have learned to use my down time in productive and godly ways. It has been a great help in my fight against temptation.

One Biblical example is Philippians 4:8-9. Our minds are powerful. Once we begin to focus on something beneficial we are shaped and molded by those thoughts. In this passage we are told to keep our mind on things that will produce godly results in our lives. I have found this to be true. If I focus on God, my family, helping others, or a useful hobby, my mind will not be drawn into lust.

You may think this is silly or simplistic, but it works. Not long ago I heard someone say God created us so that we could only focus on one thing at a time. There is a lot of truth in that statement. If my mind is focused on useful and godly things then it will not dwell on temptations. This small truth can actually be life changing if you can learn to occupy your mind with what is good. You know the old saying: garbage in equals garbage out. We know this is true in most cases. Therefore we should be able to conclude that if we can keep our minds centered on godly things, we will naturally produce godly actions. Likewise, if we keep our minds full of ungodly thoughts, we will continue to be overwhelmed and held captive.

James 1:12-15 kind of explains this from God's point of view. He knows once a temptation has sprouted within us it has the potential to grow into a sinful act. If the small seed is given the opportunity to grow, it will eventually produce ungodly fruit. That fruit is deadly.

Idleness gives the enemy an opportunity to play with our minds, to expose us to temptation, and to attack our weaknesses. I have found in my life that working hard, reading Christian books, spending time with my family or Christian friends, or anything else that keeps my mind in the right place is a wonderful weapon in my fight. On the same token, I have seen too often that idleness produces temptations, which then can lead to sinful behavior.

With this knowledge I have been able to invest my down time into useful activities. I have read more in the past few years than I ever dreamed I could. I have improved my golf game and have had some wonderful times with friends and family along the way. Perhaps the greatest blessing for me though has been writing. God has given me a desire to express my heart through writing. This has not only given me an avenue of expression, but has filled a lot of my days with useful and godly productivity. As I write, I focus in on God, what He has done in my life, what He wants me to do, His promises and warnings, and the needs of others. Writing has truly changed me.

James 1:12 has also encouraged me many times. God promises to bless those who fight against temptation. He has promised to be with those who turn their minds to godly thoughts. I know this is true. I have experienced God in new and wonderful ways as I have given my thought life to Him. As I focus on the Lord, my mind is renewed and my heart is transformed.

Another passage that comes to mind is 2 Corinthians 10:5. Our thought lives are vital in our battles to overcome our weaknesses. When we realize our minds have drifted into areas of temptation, we need to quickly rebuke the thoughts and submit them to Christ. This is not easy but is very powerful. You have to really work on this at first to develop your new habit. Before long though you will quickly recognize ungodly thoughts and willingly turn them over. As you do, you will notice your struggle's grip has begun to lose strength. You will find a new hope and joy and desire, even more freedom.

Once again I am teaching something that can be misconstrued or abused. I am not suggesting we are never supposed to relax or enjoy ourselves. God Himself took some time off. (Genesis 2:1-2) He has instructed us to rest as well. I am not proposing that you should never take a break. What I am saying is that when you do take a break, do so in a way that will help you avoid making choices that you will later regret.

The issue is we have a lot of time on our hands in our modern society. We also have more technology than we know what to do with. We have a lot of idle time, and we must learn how to handle it. You do need to have times of relaxation. God is pleased when His people rest and enjoy life. God wants us to be refreshed. Yet we must be very careful about how we spend our down times. Instead of producing blessings in our lives, they can become terrible curses, leading us deeper into the darkness.

I have really tried to start looking at everything I do and how I do it. I try to ask myself if I am spending my time wisely or actually causing more problems. When I am able to honestly examine these things I can usually determine what I need to do. If a hobby or interest is pulling me away from my goals then I should find something else to do. If my hobbies and interest are productive and help me reach my goals then I should continue to enjoy them. You might say I have learned to relax with purpose and meaning.

I have come to look at my life as a unified piece of work in progress. Instead of separating my job from my time off, my family time from my alone time, my church time from my out-of-church time, I now include them all as a part of a total project. This has really revolutionized my approach to living.

Let me explain. If I were on a job site, say building a brick wall, would I work all day, placing bricks upon bricks hoping to see the wall completed, only to spend my time off taking bricks back out of the wall? Of course not! That would be foolish. Yet we seem to do that in our personal lives. We go to church to learn and grow closer to God only to leave church to do things that prevent us from maturing in Christ. Likewise, we fight to break free from our sinful habits only to do things that continue to keep us in captivity.

Once I began to see the effects of idle time and poor use of down time, I was able to make better choices. These better choices then have resulted in less temptation, more knowledge, less guilt and shame, more fun with friends and family, and even a new passion for writing. My desires have changed, and I truly do not miss the old ones. God has even begun to fulfill these new desires, just as His word promises. (Psalm 37:4) I have more joy and peace. My life is more full and meaningful too.

The Bible warns us about the danger of idleness. (Proverbs 19:15, Ezekiel 16:49, Matthew 12:36, 1

Timothy 5:13) I have come to see the truth behind these verses. God knows idle time leads to dangerous thoughts and behavior. He has helped me to see that I can use down time for godly things that help me and others as well. This has been a great blessing in my life. I am grateful God has given me these instructions to help me remain free.

You may not face the same kind of struggle, but we can all use our down time for more godly things. I hope you will examine your life and ask God to help you see if there are hobbies or activities that are "removing your bricks." If you can identify something that is preventing you from growing and holding you back, then make a change. You have a limited amount of time in a day; spend it wisely.

Develop Discipline

Some people are born with an amazing ability to work hard, focus, and get things done. Other people are forced by circumstances to develop self-control and willpower. Yet the majority of us in our modern society have failed to mature in this area. I am one of those people who can never really stick with a game plan, see a task all the way through, or even stop eating sweets for an extended period of time. I have little willpower.

But I know self-control is a part of the fruit of the Spirit. (Galatians 5:22-23) Therefore I know, because I am a Christian, I have the Holy Spirit within me; I am now able to develop self-control due to God working to transform me from the inside out. He will enable me to mature and grow and to learn how to "possess my vessel." (1 Thessalonians 4:4) God is currently helping me gain control.

You too can learn to gain self-control and willpower. It is not easy, but it is possible if you are filled with the Holy Spirit. God desires we live in obedience; this requires discipline. God has promised to help us and empower us so we can live up to His expectation. He has not left us alone to somehow discover willpower on our own.

However I must warn you God will probably not automatically sweep away years of bad habits and laziness. He usually doesn't suddenly turn a procrastinator into a well-oiled, organized machine. Instead, He calls us to work with Him as He transforms us from within. It is a process and will require a great deal of effort and surrender on our parts. The process is intended to help us grow, mature, and learn to trust Him. If God simply made it all go away, we would never outgrow our struggles.

God wants us to be disciplined. I don't at all mean we all have to live by a day planner and function as robots. I am not teaching you to conform to a certain standard or way of life. What I am saying is that you need to learn how to make good choices and to live sensibly in this present age. (Titus 2:11-14) God wants us to be wise, to avoid sin, to use our resources wisely, and to glorify Him in all we do. As we mature and begin to live more sensibly, we will find freedom. God's way of doing things keeps us from falling and His ways are always good for us in the long run. (Romans 8:28)

We must learn to gain control of our emotions, desires, and thoughts. We have to learn to control our bodies and to submit our desires to God. This is a challenge, but it is good for us and pleasing to God.

Paul teaches us in 1 Corinthians 9:24-27 to learn to exercise self-control in all things. He uses the example of athletes training in hopes of winning a prize. He tells us in verse 27 he tries to make his body a "slave." He wants to be in control of his actions and not to be led by carnal desires.

This may be an important element in your fight for freedom. Maybe you need to learn to tell your body, "no." Maybe you need to learn to control sinful urges. Maybe you need to gain more control of your emotions. Whatever the case, you can be disciplined because of the power of the Holy Spirit that lives within you.

One final thought; do you hope a change will occur in your life or are you working towards a change in your life? Can you see the difference? You've probably heard it said in one way or another that insanity is doing the same things over and over but expecting different results. So what are you doing differently in order to get a different result?

If you want to overcome your struggle, you are going to have to make some changes in your life. I cannot identify what changes are needed in your life, but God definitely has revealed to me what I need to do. Now I must take that knowledge and apply it to my life through self-control and discipline. As I do, God produces a transformation within me.

If you hope to break free you are going to have to work on applying God's truth in your life. Lean on the Holy Spirit, but don't expect Him to do all the work for you. Train your body. Train your mind. Develop good habits that will give you the advantage over the beast within.

Remember, this will take time. You probably will not be able to make a lot of major changes all at once.

I have found it is best to focus in on one or two major changes at a time. I suggest you pray and ask God to reveal a couple of issues you need to deal with first. Once you can identify the areas where you need to begin, develop a plan and set some goals.

For instance, if you have a problem with gambling you may want to challenge yourself to not place any bets for a week. Work on this each day and celebrate with a movie or a nice meal as a reward when you hit your mark. Then move your goal up to a month of gambling free days. Record your progress and celebrate when you reach your goal.

At the same time you will need to work on supporting habits. For example, you might want to stop buying a newspaper so you will no longer thumb through the box scores and race results. You might also need to change your normal route home so you can avoid the convenience store where you used to buy lottery tickets.

As you grow in your self-control towards these supporting habits you will find a decreased desire to gamble. To help you stay motivated reward yourself and keep track of your success. Let your accountability partners know how you're doing so they can encourage you along the way. You could also put the money you are saving each week in a jar so you can literally see how your good decisions are paying off. Once you hit your goal, go on a vacation, buy yourself something nice, or open a savings account.

Once you have gained the upper hand on the gambling issue, then you can set your sights on another area that needs some attention. Take baby steps, but don't stop walking! Make real changes that will make a real difference.

I think you can see how this all works. I know it will take time, but once you begin to see results you will want to commit yourself to a more disciplined lifestyle. God will help you. Trust in the power of His Holy Spirit, and apply the truths that He reveals. You may not be the most self-controlled person today but you can develop a willpower that would make Olympic athletes proud.

Steps of Faith

One of the biggest mistakes we can make as Christians is to believe God will just simply take away all of our temptations, melt away all of our problems, or stop all of our pain instantaneously. As long as we live on this earth, we will face the common struggles of man. We will be discouraged, we will be tempted, and we will have troubles. That is a fact, and we must be willing to accept this truth or be left to live in a false reality.

The truth is if God just took it all away we would fall right back into the same struggle or perhaps one that is far worse. God wants us to learn and grow. He wants us to be transformed and matured. If He simply took away our struggle without letting us learn from it, He would actually be doing us a great harm. We don't need God to make it all go away. Instead, we need to get involved in our transformation.

God never promised we could sit back and let Him do everything, but He has asked us to join Him in the battle, He wants us to take part in our walk to freedom. There is plenty of evidence in scripture that

God will be the one who brings victory, freedom, and joy. He alone is able to set us free. Yet He wants us to work with Him. (Philippians 2:12-13) We are "co-workers" with God in our deliverance. (1 Corinthians 3:9)

We are called to guard our hearts. (Proverbs 4:23) We are told to flee from temptation. (2 Timothy 2:22) We are advised to watch out for the enemy. (1 Peter 5:8) We are also instructed to put on our battle gear and to take up arms. (Ephesians 6:10-17)

God stresses the fact over and over again in the Bible; we are supposed to join Him in the battle. He wants us to actively seek freedom. Unfortunately most of us fail to do our part. We want God to sweep His hand in our direction and simply make the bad things, such as our desires and bad habits, disappear. We are not interested in working towards victory. We, like spoiled children, want the desired results to be handed to us on a silver platter.

By the same token we can fall into the trap of trying to fix all of our problems ourselves. We may begin to depend on our own ability and efforts. This is just as dangerous. God doesn't expect us to make all the choices or to fight our battles alone. He is the one who ensures victory. We cannot depend on our own works, goodness, or self-control. If we do, we will never break free, or even worse, we could be pulled into pride and self-reliance.

Take a look at the account of David and Goliath. (1 Samuel 17) Before David arrived on the scene, Goliath had spent many days mocking God and terrorizing the army of Israel. He challenged King

Saul and the soldiers. The king and his army trembled in fear and no one dared to step out and fight the giant.

Do you suppose God wanted to give Israel the victory? Do you think God was ready to deliver His people once again from the hands of pagans? Yet Saul and his army huddled in fear, waiting for God to fix the problem. They were paralyzed and remained trapped. Until Goliath was dealt with, they wouldn't be able to advance on the enemy and quite possibly would be defeated and taken into slavery their selves.

Then David, an unknown sheep herder comes along. He was outraged by the remarks and mockery which the Philistine spewed out. He was also amazed at the lack of faith and little determination displayed by the army of Israel. David could not believe Saul or some other warrior hadn't already slain Goliath in the name of God.

We know David trusted God to the point that he stepped out to fight the giant with nothing more than a sling and five stones. When he did this, David was not counting on his own power, strength, or battle experience to give him the victory. He simply trusted God would win the battle; David was just the instrument, the weapon, in God's hands. God delivered, David killed Goliath, and the Philistines were defeated.

I have learned some powerful lessons from this amazing account of God's power and deliverance. What changed between Goliath's taunting of Israel and David's victory? Did God change? Did the circumstances change? Or did one man have the courage to step out in faith? What happened when he did?

I believe God would have slain the giant for Saul, or Eliab, or any of the Jewish warriors had they just stepped out in faith. God was waiting to defeat Goliath and the Philistines. He was ready to defend Israel. The Lord was willing to drive the enemy back, but He was waiting on someone with enough faith to take action. David's only strength was his faith. Yet, that was all God needed to give Israel a great victory.

James 2:14-26 is perhaps the most famous Bible passage when it comes to linking faith and action. The teaching is clear: faith that does not produce action is really useless and dead. If we say God wants us to help other people yet we are not willing to give from what we have, do we really believe? What good is it to say God wants to help someone, yet we withhold the very assistance God is trying to give them through His people? Likewise, what good is it to say God wants us to stop drinking, or gambling, or stealing, and yet we take no actions to end our addiction?

We are told in Hebrews chapter 11 about many who did amazing things "by faith." We can read about an amazing cast of individuals who were incredible instruments of God. Yet we see within this chapter nothing would have happened had they not acted in faith. This is such an important element in your search for freedom. God will act, but He wants you to take steps of faith. He is calling you out of the prison cell; will you step in that direction? You can remain in prison, waiting for God to come and carry you out, or you can leap to your feet and walk through the door He has already opened for you.

Perhaps the best way to look at this is that you need to move from abstract faith into practical faith. Religious ideals and theories are useless against your daily struggles. Instead you need a faith that is applicable to your everyday life. What good is a faith that produces no actions? What good is a belief that doesn't influence the choices you make everyday?

Christianity is practical, real, and authentic when you sincerely apply the truths of the Bible to your life. Acknowledging something as a good ideal or as a religious standard means nothing in reality if you don't take real steps towards applying them in your life.

How do you do this? As you read God's word and find tidbits of truth, spend some time in thought and prayer, ask God how you can practically apply that truth into your life. The answer may not come in a flash of lighting, but if you seek you will find. God will reveal real ways to apply this newly discovered truth. That may mean making a change in your life, but isn't that where faith comes in, trusting God's way is the right ways, believing submission to God's will and His truth will make a difference?

I cannot stress enough the importance of moving from an abstract, idealistic faith into a practical, applicable faith. When you read God's word and listen to sermons, and pray, look for truths you can actually put into practice. This is life changing!

God has delivered me. God has brought joy, hope, and freedom into my life. But it has not happened overnight or by accident. God didn't suddenly wipe away my dark desires. He didn't simply brush away all the temptations. However, He did promise to show me a way out of the darkness, and to deliver me if I would follow Him.

I have had to take some drastic but necessary steps along my path to freedom. I have had to put into practice what I have come to believe. For example, because I believe what I see and hear has a tremendous affect on my thought life, I try to limit my exposure to any form of sexually suggestive music. This means I have basically stopped listening to anything but "Christian" music. I have a favorite radio station which plays contemporary Christian music, it has been a Godsend.

It has taken years to form this habit, but now I truly can't stand to listen to the sexually explicit messages in country, or rock, or other forms of music. I am no longer comfortable with the messages they contain. God has changed my desires. However, it did require some discipline and self-control on my part. I worked with God to form a new, life changing habit. Now the music I listen to glorifies God, and never leads me into temptation! Instead, it strengthens me, encourages me, and reminds me of my Savior. He is glorified, and I am walking in freedom.

Another example is how my wife and I try to be very careful about what we watch. At one time we would rent our children a "kids" movie and pop it in the VCR. Once they had watched their video, we would send them off to bed so we could watch a "grown up movie." Once I began to deal with my problem, Val and I agreed that if the kids could not watch the movie with us then we probably didn't need to watch it either. This has been challenging and, yes, we have had to stop some movies halfway through and return them without finishing the show. Yes, we have missed some "blockbuster" movies, but I have also avoided a great amount of temptation in the process. (Plus we have set a positive example for our children.) Now television shows and movies I was once comfortable with seem raunchy and no longer catch my attention. Once again God has changed my desires, but it required my willingness to make a change, and the support of Val. Together we made a wise move that has helped not only us but our girls as well. We have eliminated a source of negative influence and gained more family time. What a trade off!

God will change the desires of your heart. He will set you on a new path of freedom, but He wants you to join Him in the transformation. That is what I learned from 2 Timothy 2:20-22. God wants to use me for good works. Therefore, I must make an effort to be useful and willing to submit to His commands. If I will do my part, God will do amazing things in me, through me, for me, and with me. He will do the same for you. Take steps of faith. Put into practice what you already believe to be true. When His light shines upon the path, step out and follow as He leads, trusting in His faithfulness.

You Don't Fight Alone

Recently I was studying the book of Joshua. It was the first time I had ever really delved deeply into this Old Testament scripture. As I read and prayed over chapter ten, I was overwhelmed by God's willingness to fight for His people.

Let me set up the scene. God had been faithful and had given Israel the Promised Land. But there was one problem: someone else already lived there! The land was filled with ungodly people and as Israel moved into the area God had promised Abraham, they faced a lot of armed resistance. At one point five kings gathered together to wage a war against Israel and those who had made peace with them. Moses had turned over the command post to Joshua before the Israelites crossed over the Jordan River, and the new leader now faced growing fears, and five angry kings.

I was moved deeply by the events as they unfolded in Joshua 10:6-11. Messengers were sent to Joshua. The enemy was attacking, and the people of Gibeon needed reinforcements. Joshua could have aban-

doned the Gibeonites considering they had tricked
Israel into forming a partnership. He could have fled
from the battle, but instead rallied the troops and
marched against the attacking kings. Why did Joshua
do this? Was it based on the strength of his troops or
his own military prowess?

His courage and actions were not based on
anything human. The way he responded was based
solely on his faith in God. God had made Joshua a
promise, and the Israelite leader believed God would
fight for them and give them the victory. (Joshua 1:1-
9) This was his strength. This was Joshua's hope.
It was the only reason he was willing to lead the
Israelite troops against the five kings. Joshua acted
on his faith in God. He applied what he knew to be
true: God would fight for Israel.

I gained so much insight from this passage.
First of all, Joshua knew the promises of God, and
he claimed those promises. The word of God was
more than just something to put on a birthday card
or calendar. Joshua believed God was faithful, and
he was willing to step out in action based solely on
God's word. His faith was not abstract but real. His
belief in God was not just idealistic. It influenced his
life and produced godly actions. Joshua had a practical faith.

The other thing I noticed, God had made the
promise to protect and deliver Israel, but He did not
act upon that promise until Joshua rallied the troops
and marched against the five kings. Just as David had
to pick up the stones, place one in his sling, and then
literally rush up against Goliath so, too, Joshua had

to literally take a step of faith. God promised to give them the victory, but they had to work with Him and trust Him enough to take action. Once they did, the battle was already won.

This really hit me hard. For so long I wanted God to do all the work. I believed "in Him" but did not always "believe Him." I trusted God enough to ask for salvation, but never really trusted Him enough to step out in faith and fight against the beast within me. I wanted God to set me free, but without taking up a sword of my own. You might say my faith at that point was still idealistic and not yet practical, or you could say it was immature and untested.

You may know what I am talking about. You may have wondered why God has never delivered you from the enemy. Perhaps it is because you have never stepped out in faith and fought against the attacks of the enemy, trusting God would give you the victory.

Now that I know God more personally and have learned to lean on His promises, I can step out and fight along side Him, instead of shrinking in fear. The truth is I could never overcome my struggle under my own power. I can never defeat the enemy on my own, but I don't fight alone, and neither do you.

God has promised to set us free. God has promised to destroy those who come up against His people. Do you believe this? Do you claim the promises of God like Joshua did? Do you trust Him enough to grab your sword and face the enemy head on?

In my years as a minister and through many conversations, I have discovered most people do not believe God is fighting with them. When they read the promises of the Bible, they believe those words are meant for someone else; anyone but them. Instead of finding courage, and strength, and direction, they remain in fear and sin.

When I was younger I never really understood the truth about God's love and power. For so long I never grasped the concept that the promises of God are for me too! This knowledge has not only given me hope but has given me ammunition as well. When the enemy attacks, I can boldly proclaim the promises of God. When I am under attack and the troops of temptation are marching against me, I now have something to fight back with. Instead of running in fear, I can call upon God and know He is not only fighting with me, but has already promised me a victory. I can win! I can live in purity! So can you!

We can also look to Jesus to see how He handled the battles He faced while on earth. In John 16:32-33, we can see that Jesus knew God was with Him as He prepared to face crucifixion. Jesus knew the disciples would abandon Him for a time and that He would have to face the cross without them. Yet Jesus declared He was not alone! He knew God would never abandon Him. He knew He could rest in the fact that God promised to raise Him up from the grave.

This was all Jesus had to hang on to, but it was enough. Jesus knew He didn't face the cross alone. He knew God had promised to pull Him through. Do we trust God in that way?

Hebrews 12:1-3 is a battle cry to all Believers. We can look to Jesus and follow His example. He kept His eyes focused on the promises of God and trusted God would never abandon Him. This gave Him the strength and courage to face the cross, looking forward to the "joy" that was to follow the pain, expecting fully that God would carryout every word He had promised.

You do not fight alone, God has not abandoned you. Just remember we have to trust in the unseen. (Hebrews 11:1-3) We worship a God who is Spirit. (John 4:24) Therefore, we will not always feel Him, or see Him, or hear Him, but we can trust He is here, fighting with us. This truth brings hope, courage, and the will to go on against all odds.

That is what happened in 2 Kings 6:11-23. Elisha was surrounded by the Aramean army. The prophet was unarmed and alone, except for his attendant. As dawn broke, the servant went outside only to be stricken with fear as he looked upon the rows of chariots and warriors encircling their camp.

Naturally Elisha's attendant was overcome with fear; he was hopeless and didn't know what to do. Yet the prophet was calm, he knew there was no reason to panic because he could see the spiritual truth; they were not alone!

Elisha prayed and asked God to open the servant's eyes so he too could see the truth. The Lord responded to Elisha's request and gave the attendant a glimpse into the spiritual realm. When He did, the man was able to see a massive army; the hills were full of horses and chariots of fire. God went on to deliver the two godly men from the enemy.

As I was studying this passage, I noticed an important spiritual truth that also shows up in the New Testament as well. 2 Kings 6:16 mention that the men of God had a greater army with them than the enemy had. This same idea is seen in Romans 8:31 and 1 John 4:4. These verses tell us we have great and amazing resources as children of God. Not only is God with us, but so are His angels! The power of the enemy is nothing compared to the authority and might of God.

Romans 8:32-39 goes on to say that nothing can separate us from the love of God. If you are a Christian, you have resources and protection far beyond our human reason. This is one of the great truths of the Bible. We therefore can rest and know we do not fight alone.

So as you battle against the darkness, as you wage war on temptation, and as you combat sin in your life, fall back on the promises of God. He has not left us as orphans, He as not forgotten about us. He fights with us and for us. Just as He delivered Joshua and Elisha, God will deliver you.

Blessings

$\vdash$

G od will bless you when you seek Him. This is a truth that is displayed from Genesis to Revelation. God pours His favor and blessings upon those who walk in faith and obey His commandments. (Deuteronomy 11:26-28, Psalm 115:9-15, Matthew 6:33, Colossians 3:16-25, Revelation 22:14)

God blesses those who seek Him and obey His commands because of who He is: loving, kind, and generous. Likewise, God cannot pour His favor and blessings upon those who walk in disobedience because of who He is: just, holy, and righteous. (1 Samuel 12:14-15, Jeremiah 5:21-25) It would go against His nature as God to reward those who rebel and disobey Him. Would we even want to love and serve a God who offered His favor to those who lived in opposition to His commands? What kind of God would He be if He treated obedience and disobedience with indifference?

The Bible unquestionably teaches us God blesses those who are obedient. This truth is often lost in our modern teaching of grace. We are definitely saved by grace through faith in Jesus. God is also slow to anger, and quick to forgive, and to restore us when we repent. His grace and loving kindness are without measure. These are the truths that draw us to God and compel us to seek His mercy. His grace is amazing and beyond our understanding, but is it possible we have used His grace as an excuse to live in sin?

I love God's grace, but I once lived as if obedience meant nothing to my Lord. I guess I reasoned that if I was forgiven and my sins were remembered no more, then obedience really didn't matter. I also knew God would forgive me if I asked, so I assumed I could sin, and then just plead for mercy. I don't think I ever purposefully thought this through or plotted out my rebellion, but this was basically the way I looked at obedience. Why bother if it doesn't matter to God! In other words, I thought I could take advantage of grace.

Through Bible study and prayer, the Lord has revealed to my heart that He still demands obedience, not for salvation, but for other important reasons. He ties His favor and blessings to obedience. (Hebrews 11:6, James 1:25) We are less useful to Him if we live in rebellion and sin. (2 Timothy 2:20-22) Disobedience hinders or quenches the Holy Spirit. (Ephesians 4:30) Not obeying the commands that have been revealed in the Bible puts us in opposition to God. (James 4:4) Sin and rebellion open us up to the attacks of the enemy. (Proverbs 7:24-27, 1 Peter 5:8)

The Bible also contains many wonderful promises of God's blessings for those who seek Him and obey

His commands. God has even graciously promised to bless us with forgiveness and restoration when we confess our sins. But at the same time, He has given us sharp warnings about living in rebellion and opposition to His revealed instructions for our lives.

Ezekiel 14:6-8 is one example. When the people of Israel rejected God, and began to worship idols and perform sinful acts, the Lord rebuked them. He told the people plainly in verse eight He would set His face against anyone who would not repent. Now remember, these are God's chosen people! He loved them and had made them great promises, yet He didn't take their sin lightly. 1 Corinthians 10:6 tells us to learn from Israel's mistakes. If God would not tolerate their sin, why should we believe He will tolerate ours?

We need to understand the wonderful promises of God, but at the same time we need to take these warnings seriously. I am not suggesting that good things only happen to good people. Nor am I saying that only bad things happen to bad people. The Bible clearly denounces this kind of theology. (Matthew 5:45) Yet at the same time, we know God gives special favor to those who seek His will and obey His commands. (Proverbs 12:2, Matthew 6:33, Hebrews 11:6, James 1:22-25)

Most of my life I chose to ignore these deep truths. In reality, I never really thought much about how my actions affected my relationship with God and His ability to bless me. I was never really taught about the connection between seeking God, obeying His word, and the amazing blessings He has promised to pour upon those who love Him. I was mostly taught about Jesus forgiving our sins and not much else.

I am risking the possibility I will be misunderstood. I know there are people who teach a "name it and claim it" gospel. That is not at all what I am doing. However, I am proclaiming that God has given us specific promises of blessings and warnings. The Bible teaches God that will give special favor to those who desire to obey Him with all of their hearts. The Bible also teaches that God gives special favor and blessings to those who are "doers" of the word. I believe this is an overwhelming truth that is consistent throughout the Old and New Testaments because it is a fundamental characteristic of God.

Take, for example, the words of Deuteronomy 11:26-28. These verses clearly show us that the blessings are contingent upon obedience, and the same is true for the curse. Disobedience will result in turning away from God, which leads to rebuke and discipline.

Malachi 3:8-12 gives us the same lesson. If we fail to follow the revealed word of God, we will face a rebuke and unpleasant consequences. On the other hand, God will open up the doors of heaven and pour out blessings upon those who trust Him enough to obey His word. God has given us the free will to choose which kind of person we will be and how we will respond to these truths.

Our obedience to God also affects our families. Psalm 103:15-18 declares the truth: if we truly want the Lord to bless our children, then we need to live in obedience. What we do impacts not only our lives, but our spouses, and especially our children as well. I love my daughters and only want the best for them. How then, can I live in a way that would hinder God's blessings in their lives? How can I choose to ignore this truth and continue to live in the darkness? I have said often that I would give my life for my daughters and I mean it from the depths of my soul. Can I say the same thing about surrendering my sinful habits? Will I give up my selfish desires for my children's sakes?

Hebrews 11:6 is a revealing verse as well. God rewards those who seek Him! Even Revelation 22:14 speaks this truth into our lives. God blesses those who obey His commandments. Scripture is full of these kinds of promises. When we turn our knowledge of the truth into actions of faith, we live out the truth of the Bible, and then God blesses us. We do not serve our God in vain! He is a rewarder of those who seek Him!

On the other hand, James 4:1-4 makes some pretty powerful points about the consequences of living in a sinful way. Clearly, relationships, prayers, and blessings are affected by sin. If we choose to live in sin, we are choosing to live in opposition to God. This gets my attention. I have read enough of the Bible to know I do not want to oppose God Almighty!

Hebrews 12:4-11 has been an eye opening passage for me also. Often times we forget being a Christian means we are now accountable to God as His children. When we receive His grace, and are given eternal life, we are adopted and granted a place within His household. With this amazing blessing, we are also brought into accountability, and accountability is meaningless without discipline. It would be no more than an empty threat and therefore useless. The Bible clearly displays that God doesn't make empty threats!

God's word describes His discipline as temporary but painful. Discipline, real godly discipline, is not pain free. In fact, the Bible tells us God's discipline brings sorrow. It will hurt. It will not be pleasant. This is real, get-your-attention discipline. It is the same kind of discipline that a loving parent uses to help teach a child.

Please understand that the discipline of God is a sign of His love. He doesn't hate us or refuse to receive us if we repent. Out of love God will get our attention. He desires that we come back to Him and trust Him enough to obey His commands. When we choose to live in rebellion, God doesn't "turn His back on us," but rather "sets His face against us." Do you see the difference? God is not rejecting us but is trying to get our attention through discipline.

This brings to my mind a memory from my childhood. My brothers, sisters, and I have joked many times about my Dad's famous "glare." When we would get in trouble all Dad had to do was give us the glare, we knew we had been warned. We understood what he meant, and he usually never had to take it any further.

Though I didn't appreciate it at the time, I am now thankful Dad disciplined us instead of turning his back on us. If he had ignored our fussing and fighting, we would have become spoiled and unruly children. Our house would have been chaotic and our lives would have turned out much differently. He could have turned his back on us when we misbehaved. He could have chosen to let us do whatever we wanted. He could have rejected us when we disappointed him. Instead, he would sometimes "set his face against us" so we would straighten up and obey the rules. I praise God for my Dad and his firm but loving hand. I needed to be trained up. I needed to be taught how to act. I needed to learn to obey rules. His discipline, though painful at the time, has helped me and truly been a wonderful blessing in my life.

Looking back, I know I could have avoided the glare by following the rules to begin with. I know I could have also avoided the more painful encounters too, had I heeded the initial warnings. Likewise, we don't have to go through God's disciplinary actions. If we walk in obedience and do what we know is pleasing to God, He will bless us and have no reason to rebuke us. Our relationship with God will flourish, and our lives will produce godliness. Obeying God produces righteousness and opens up the doors of heaven. Obedience puts us in a place that allows God to bless us. Disobedience opens us up to discipline and painful consequences. We make the choices.

Once again I want to stress the fact I am not saying that if you obey God to the best of your ability nothing bad will ever happen in your life. The Bible never teaches that if you obey God, you will win the lottery, or never face a financial crisis or personal loss. That is not at all what God promises. But what

I am saying is that obedience puts you in a place to be blessed and keeps you from the need to be disciplined, and instead opens your life up to the favor and blessings of God.

Sometimes God's greatest blessings are difficulties in our lives. Sometimes God's greatest gifts to us are hardships. At the time we usually don't see that, but later praise Him for allowing us to hurt and face harsh realities. So please never let your circumstances be your conscience. Learn the truth about God's commands and obey them no matter what you face. This is pleasing to God, and He will reward you for your faithfulness.

These are serious revelations. I hope you take this teaching to heart and really contemplate your life choices. God cannot pour out His blessings and favor on those who live in opposition to His commandments. On the other hand, God loves to open the doors of heaven and to shower blessings upon those who seek Him. Which do you desire? Which will bring true joy and satisfaction in life? Do you live in a way that allows God to bless you?

Tests

We all face temptations. We all have weaknesses. We all are given opportunities to follow God. That is what test and temptations are really all about. They are opportunities to follow Him, and obtain the great promises of the Bible.

I have begun to look at my struggle in a different light over the years. I used to think God had cursed me with a horrible problem. Now I see it is my own sinful nature that draws me towards lust and not God. (James 1:12-18) It is sin that calls my name and beckons me to give in just one more time. The enemy pushes my buttons, pulls the strings of our society, and tries to draw me into the dungeon. Yet it is my sinful nature that presents the biggest problem; it desires the evil, it wants to be satisfied.

Though God has the power to completely flush away all my sinful desires He does not. That used to bother me. I often questioned God, wondering why He would allow me to desire sinful things when He knew I wanted to follow Him. For so long I struggled with such thoughts. Now, I have come to a new and vital understanding. Simply put, if there is not test of faith, I cannot be found faithful. If there is no room for a bad choice, I cannot make a good choice. If there is no opportunity for disobedience, I cannot decide to be obedient. God, therefore, has allowed temptations and trials to remain in my life so I can choose to follow Him by faith, trusting that His way is the best.

There is one important element about God that we must be careful not to overlook: God uses evil for good! (Genesis 50:20) I have mentioned this already, but must once again bring it to the forefront. One of the most amazing characteristics of God is the fact He is above all things and can turn evil into good. Please do not misunderstand this, God does not approve of evil, and God will not bless evil. Instead, He will use evil for His good and for the good of those who seek Him. Because He is holy, we know God can and will not bless what is evil. However, He can and will use what is evil for His good purpose and to accomplish His overall plan. There is a big difference.

For example, Acts 3:13-15 points out that God used the sin of man to bring salvation to the world. By killing Jesus, the Jews and Romans fulfilled the prophecies God had ordained from the beginning of time. (Hebrews 4:3, Revelation 13:8) This dreadful act of man ushered in the mighty grace of God. Once Jesus was slain, God was able to raise Him from the dead, overcoming sin and death, and opening up the door of salvation to this lost and dying world. (Romans 6:8-11) God blessed the whole world through the sin of those who crucified Jesus, in alignment with His merciful and loving nature. But He did not bless those individuals who committed the shameful brutalities and mockeries. To do so would have contradicted His holy nature.

The greatest work of God that has ever occurred happened by the hands of sinful man: Jesus, the Son of God, was crucified. The perfect, sinless Son of God was slain, offering up His own life for ours. (Hebrews 9:12-15) This is our hope. This is the foundation of our faith. This is Christianity. The blood of Jesus shed for the remission of our sins.

In this truth, God displayed not only His sovereignty and grace, but His willingness to use sin for good as well. Though God does not cause us to sin or endorse sin, He is more than able to use evil for His ultimate plan, and for our ultimate good.

With this knowledge, I can look upon passages like 1 Peter 1:3-9, and find strength to endure temptations. In this set of verses we can see that God uses temptations and trials to test our faith. In other words: the way we respond to the hardships of life and the enticement of sin, reveals our commitment to Him. As we face the realities of life and the allure of lust, greed, or pride, we have the opportunity to declare our faith in God. As we overcome our struggles, and live out His commandments faithfully, we bring glory and honor to Him, and at the same time open our lives up to receive the blessings He has promised to pour upon those who seek Him. (Hebrews 11:6)

This has been another life changing revelation for me. As I face the tests of hardships, difficult choices, and temptations, I now see the true potential of the moment: I can give into my own desires, or I can stand firm in my faith by obeying His commands, trusting in His promises, and anticipating the good that will result from it all. Which choice will God bless? Which choice will glorify His name? Which choices will be worth it in the long run?

God does not leave temptations and hardships in our lives because He hates us or to catch us in a mistake. God is not waiting for us to mess up so He can unleash His wrath upon a disobedient child. Rather, He allows trials and difficulties to remain as opportunities to follow Him. Therefore, tests become potential proofs of our faith, and open our lives up to the possibility of His blessings and favor.

Remember the Bible assures Believers "all things work for the good of those who love Him." (Romans 8:28) This is an invaluable truth that can help us overcome when life is hard or when temptations seem to come at us from all sides. We need to always keep in mind that even temptations and trails work to the good of those who love Him. When we obey and follow Him, tests produce joy, peace, blessings, and a testimony of our faith. When we stumble and fall they produce a lesson and rebuke, which we need, and can potentially bless us, if we learn from our mistakes. (Hebrews 12:7-11)

Hebrews 12:1-2 reminds us that we can look back at those who have fought the battle before us and even to Christ Himself as an example. The faithful people mentioned in Hebrews 11 acted in faith, believing it was worth it to serve God. Likewise, Jesus endured the cross, looking towards the joy that was set before Him.

Our Lord knew He was not going to suffer in vain. Not only was His death the price of atonement for our sins, but it also proved His faithfulness to the Father. His willingness to die on the cross gave us the opportunity to be forgiven, but it also verified His absolute trust in God, and His commitment to God. Jesus then was ushered into heaven, where He now sits in glory. He obtained the promises by living in complete obedience to His Father's will. (Philippians 2:5-11)

Even though Jesus looked forward to the promises God had given Him, it was not easy to endure the tests He faced as a man. His time in the garden of Gethsemane proves that well enough. (Matthew 26:36-44) Jesus was also tempted to seek His own safety and comfort and pleasure on many other occasions. (Matthew 4:1-11, Mark 15:29-31, Hebrews 4:15) Yet He kept His eyes focused on the promises of God, looking forward to the day every promise would be fulfilled. He believed it would be worth it to obey, and He was willing to do whatever it took, even dying on the cross, in order to obtain the promises before Him. Jesus truly believed God would reward Him!

If Jesus was tempted, we can be certain we will face tests also. Temptations will come and difficult times are a common part of life on earth. God doesn't take away all discomfort and pain. Instead, He uses it all for our good. He uses them as opportunities to test our faith. We then have to choose whether we will stand firm or give in. This in turn determines what we will gain (or lose) from the tests. (1 Corinthians 3:10-15, 2 John 1:8)

God is not cruel. He is not trying to push us beyond our limits. Instead, the Bible tells us in 1 Corinthians 10:13, He will never allow us to be tested beyond our ability to withstand. God promises us within this verse that He will always give us an avenue of escape. This brings me great hope. I know with His help and my commitment and willingness to remain pure, I can break free. I have learned to claim this promise regularly. It truly is empowering!

The Bible also tells us if we resist and endure for a short time the trial will pass or the temptation will subside. (James 4:7, 1 Peter 5:10) In other words, we will not have to resist forever. The urge will fade, the desire will diminish, and in its place, we will find joy in the knowledge we withstood and obeyed.

Once we have endured we can then expect the fulfillment of the promises we clung to so tightly. (Hebrews 6:13-18, James 1:12) By faith we obey. By faith we endure. By faith we obtain the promises of God. Please do not let this important fact pass you by.

With these truths in mind, I have tried to identify a very practical way to face trials and temptations. In doing so, I have come up with these simple but powerful suggestions to help you face your own personal struggles.

First, learn the truth and expose the lies. If you are tempted to give in to a moment of pleasure, examine the facts so you can determine if the payoff is worth the pain. Sin usually promises a quick, self-centered moment of gratification or some other type of reward. To defend against this, ask yourself if it is truly worth it, will you be glad you made the choice an hour, a day or a month later? Will people you love be glad you made the choice?

Second, look deeper. Take a minute to determine, to the best of your ability, what you believe God's view of the matter would be. Ask yourself, "What does the Bible state about the situation or choice?" Will your actions allow God to pour His blessings and favor upon you? Would you follow through on your desire if you were in church or around someone you respected? What long-term effects could result if you make the wrong choice? Just hesitating for a moment and allowing God time to prompt and guide you is a powerful tool in itself. He has promised to guide you. Will you follow?

Third, examine God's promises. Ask yourself if giving in will help you obtain the promises of God or instead keep you from enjoying the rewards of faithfulness? Try to remind yourself of God's promise to bless those who seek Him, and don't forget to think about His warnings to rebuke us as well. Take these things seriously, dwell upon them, and let His truth guide your decision making process.

Finally, look for a way out. Remember, God always promises an escape or a solution. You don't have to give in. You don't have to go back. You don't have to live in guilt and shame. The Bible guarantees us that there is an escape. The question then becomes, will you look for the exit sign?

I hope I do not mislead anyone by giving the impression we should look for temptations or bring hardship upon ourselves in order to show God how much we trust Him. This would be foolish, and could possibly be the cause of great pain and harm in our lives. Nor am I suggesting we should create a circumstance in order to somehow gain God's approval. Instead, we should avoid temptation, and do our best to prevent hardships by living out the instructions of God's word each day. It is always far better to faithfully avoid temptations in the first place. There will be plenty of trials and opportunities to obey in the face of temptation without creating our own problems.

This new understanding of my sinful nature and the overwhelming goodness of God has helped me tremendously. Instead of fearing my next battle with darkness, I now see it as a natural part of life, and I view it as an opportunity to please my God, and to display my faith. When I resist the sinful desires that attack me, I know it's worth it, and that God sees my efforts, and my sincere trust in His goodness. This has given me great strength and courage to endure. I have come to fully believe that we do not serve God in vain. Everytime I obey, He sees and rewards. Everytime I resist evil, He is glorified. Everytime I avoid sin, He is pleased. Everytime He sets me free, I find new joy in my salvation, and that is far greater than any amount of guilty pleasure.

Day by Day

A s I was writing this book a friend and I were talking about her son's struggles. He was a good kid that has now drifted away from his convictions. He wants to change. He wants to stop living in a way he knows is neither right nor beneficial. As we discussed the general idea behind this book, she made a comment that has stuck with me: her son needed something to help him fight day-by-day. He needed real hands on, practical help to get him through the week.

The truth is we all need this kind of help. I know I have felt so trapped and desperate at times and believed there was no way to break out of the prison I found myself in. I wanted and needed help, but didn't know where to turn. It took years and lots of missteps to realize I needed to take purposeful steps of freedom each day. As I made better choices one day at a time, I began to see weeks and then months of godly living. I began to see that God was changing me from the inside out. With that in mind, I want to provide a few Biblical pieces of advice that can be used daily to help you overcome your own personal struggles.

The first will probably be so obvious you will quickly skip over it in hopes of a magic cure. There are no "quick fixes" here. The truth is that Bible reading and prayer are invaluable and can never be replaced by anything else. God has blessed us with His word, communication through prayer, and His Holy Spirit to guide us. Yet so often we overlook and ignore these valuable tools. Instead, we seek a self-help program that we hope will set us free with little personal effort. We seek to no avail, and wind up in deeper depression and doubt.

I encourage you to develop realistic Bible reading and prayer habits. You don't have to spend hours a day in reading and prayer time, but you do need to be serious about it. God has given you tools to learn more about Him and His desires for your life. He has also blessed you with the ability to communicate with Him. Finally, He has empowered every Christian with His Holy Spirit to help guide and comfort us as we pray and read. The problem is we seldom invest our time and energy into discovering the richness of these treasures. I hope after reading this book you will develop a realistic and consistent prayer and Bible reading time in your life. It truly will transform you from within. It is slow and requires commitment, but these weapons are invaluable in your fight for freedom.

We live in a society that values instant results. We have become accustomed to microwaveable meals and high speed internet. Anything that takes time, extra effort, and long-term commitment garners little interest. We are an impatient people and really struggle with self-control and healthy lifestyles. Perhaps this is why most people never develop quality Bible reading and prayer habits. We want easy answers and we want them right now!

The fact is quick fixes and magic formulas don't work; they usually only cause more heartache and pain. I hope you can see by now, you are going to have to work at this and know that it will take time. If you hope to find true freedom, you are going to have to make a real effort to learn more about the Bible and spend real time in prayer.

Personally, I have switched my way of looking at Bible study. I no longer wait until I am in a crisis to begin trying to find answers. I have come to realize that a few minutes invested in reading the Bible and praying everyday changes me. I have noticed my knowledge of God has grown along the way. My understanding of who God is and what He has done for us has increased dramatically. Also, the overall picture of the Bible has come more into focus, and best of all, every once in awhile I will come across a fresh revelation. These special words of encouragement or instruction then become powerful weapons in my life. They change me. They strengthen me. They help me walk in freedom.

God will do the same thing for you if you will seek Him in faith. This means believing in the possibility that God can and will open your eyes to something He wants you to know. This is where your faith becomes practical: believing in this possibility enough to spend time reading and praying regularly. Do you believe in the promises of God enough to seek them out? (Jeremiah 29:11-14, Matthew 7:7-11) Will you believe enough to wait on God's timing? Will you seek until you find?

God promises to reveal things to those who seek Him. Therefore, I believe if you seek a revelation, you will eventually receive one. When God does give you a "word" or a fresh revelation of truth, write it down. We often hear God through Bible study, prayer, sermons, or by reading a book, but then quickly let the truth fade from our hearts. You might try developing a list of scriptures and truths that you can glance over daily. (I have one taped inside the front cover of my Bible, I try to read and reflect on at least one of these each day. This has been a great help in my daily walk to purity.) God's word is powerful and will transform you, but you have to learn to apply it in your life, and this is an efficient and helpful way to do it. You need to know personally what God has promised to do for those who call upon His name. You need to learn and respect the warnings that God clearly out-lines in His word. You need a steady supply of truth to fill your lamp.

Another area that needs constant attention is community worship and learning. You need church! You need Bible study times with other Christians. You need the insight and wisdom of other people and gifted teachers. You need to praise and worship God with other Believers, and you need to be a part of a Christian community.

This is a truth you can either embrace or run from. But remember, the choice you make will greatly affect your life. If you choose to stay away from church and other Christian activities, you will miss out on fresh truths and quickly forget old ones. However, if you commit to attending a church and other Christian events, you will be strengthened and inspired regularly.

God never intended for us to be "lone rangers." We are meant to grow and learn together. We need each other. Find a solid Bible-based church and get plugged in. Surround yourself with authentic Christian friends. Attend Bible studies or small groups when possible, and expect God to speak to your heart. You need others to support, comfort, teach, and even rebuke you from time to time. Without the love, support, encouragement, and guidance of a community of Believers, you are vulnerable. Outside of the Christian community you are an easy target for the enemy, and when you try to walk alone it is almost impossible to pick yourself up when you fall. (Ecclesiastes 4:10)

You don't have to be at church everytime the doors are open. You don't have to spend every evening at a Bible study. Yet you need to at least make these things a part of your life. Think about it, can you really expect to be shaped and molded by God if you never come into contact with Biblical teaching and corporate worship?

The next obvious, but so seldom practiced, good habit is the need to flee from immorality. God warns us to flee from those things that cause us to stumble.

So often though, we set ourselves up for failure. Instead, we need to take action!

Step away from the friends, places, or circumstances that lead you into temptation. If you struggle with lust, then flee from internet usage. Use blockers and other technologies to help fight your temptation if you have to be on-line, and you can ask someone to hold you accountable. Also, avoid watching movies or television shows that get your motor running. You get the idea. Fight back against temptation! Run from those things that try to hold you in prison. If you resist temptation for just one day, you have won a battle. If you resist temptation for seven days in a row, you have made a great advance against the enemy. If you resist temptation for thirty days, you have achieved a great victory. Remember, if you are a Christian, you don't fight alone. Tap into the power that is available to you as a child of God. You can do this!

We know it is not easy to change old habits or to walk away from harmful relationships, yet these changes are so important. Once again, you need to learn to apply your faith to the situation. What do you know and believe about God? Does He love you? Will God provide you with new friends and relationships? Will He meet all of your needs if you are seeking Him? Will the Lord help you find joy in new hobbies and interest? If you believe God loves you, and wants the best for you, and that He will give you what you need, then step out in faith and flee from those things that keep you enslaved.

Everyday commit yourself to making wise choices based on what you know about God and His word. Let scripture be your standard. Make your choices based on the facts and not on your emotions or desires. (Can you see why learning more about the Bible is so helpful? The more you know about God and His instructions for life, the greater your chances of making the right choices daily.)

Another thing you can do day by day is to acknowledge your sin when you fall. Through Bible study, prayer, listening to sermons, talking to friends, and by other forms of Christian learning, you will be confronted with your sins. God will reveal areas of your life that need some attention. When He does, face the beast. Admit who you are and why you chose to sin. Acknowledge your mistake instead of trying to cover it up. Confession is always a vital first step to freedom.

God knows you, but do you know yourself? You are not hiding anything from God. You may try to cover up and justify sin in your life, but He sees it all. Do you believe this? If yes, the question then becomes: will you admit you have a problem? Will you confess your sin when He brings it to your attention? Be honest with yourself and let God heal you from the inside out. You will never overcome sin if you are not willing to daily confess your mistakes and seek His grace as often as you need it.

Repent and confess your mistake, and receive the Lord's overwhelming love. If you mess up, don't give up. Take His hand and let Him restore you and comfort you. Whatever you do, please never let a mistake drive you from God. Rather, let it drive you to Him. God is full of compassion and mercy. He wants to restore, heal, and bless you. Receive His mercy. Remember, even if He sets His face against you, He will not turn His back on you. God responds to authentic repentance and will forgive us when we ask.

Also, remember to fight idleness. One of the great revelations in my life was the fact that idleness increased my weakness and created opportunities to slip into sin. I have learned to find useful, beneficial, and meaningful things to fill my time. During my spare time, I exercise, play golf with my family, read, write, or work around the house. I can relax and have a good time, but I need to defend my heart against idleness. This is a powerful weapon in my life each day. I have found that my level of temptation is often equal to my level of idleness. Filling my extra time with godly activity has really reduced the desire to slip into sin. Plus, the time I have spent wisely has produced great benefits as well. I am closer to my wife and kids, I have gained more knowledge, learned to express myself better, and I am also in better shape. My tendency to fall into temptation has been replaced with wonderful blessings in my life. Isn't God good!

Don't give yourself an opportunity to dwell upon ungodliness. Keep your mind occupied with worthy thoughts, hobbies, or other interests. If you develop productive and godly habits, you will find that your temptations diminish. Ask God to help you form new healthy and beneficial interest. Then make a daily effort to avoid periods of idleness. When you realize you have slipped into idleness, do something about it. I am not proposing that you must always be busy or working. Relaxing is important, but you can find productive and beneficial ways to rest and enjoy life.

To get started you might examine your daily routine and try to identify areas that tend to lead you into temptation or failure. Ask yourself if your down time is productive and beneficial, is it helping you or keeping you bound in sin? Does your time off produce any positive effects in your life? You can also try to determine if God is pleased with and able to bless your hobbies and interest. If you will honestly answer these questions, you should be headed down the path to freedom. Remember, the Holy Spirit will help you analyze your life and form new habits. You are not in this alone.

Finally, praise God. Continue to acknowledge all God has done for you. Everyday celebrate your victories, and praise Him for saving you. Even if you have had a bad day and have made bad choices, thank Him for His grace and mercy. Praise Him for His kindness and longsuffering. On the same token, rejoice and give thanks everytime you win a battle. Honor Him and glorify His name everytime He helps you take a step further away from your past mistakes. One way to do this is to tell a friend or loved one, let them know God is at work in your life. The more you acknowledge God and give thanks, the greater your faith will grow. We all need to daily praise and honor God. This in itself is a powerful way to live in freedom.

Praising and honoring God helps us to stay focused. It also reminds us that apart from God, we are unable to live in purity and to walk in righteousness. True praise and worship humbles us and reminds us of the amazing love and grace of God.

If you need some help with this, try reading through the Psalms and identify a few that touch you. This will not work for everyone, but has been helpful in my own life. Sometimes a Psalm will inspire a tremendous amount of gratitude and praise in my heart. You can also try listening to some of your favorite praise songs or other Christ-centered music. As you listen and sing along, you may be drawn into a place of adoration and thanksgiving. Then let your heart rejoice as you praise Him. These are just a few suggestions. Seek out your own avenues of worship. Find the ones that inspire you.

As you praise God, use your time wisely, confess your sins, flee immorality, attend church, and read the Bible and pray. God will use these daily activities to transform you. These are real, practical examples of what you can do each day to find strength. They may seem simplistic, but that doesn't negate their power. If you can develop discipline in these areas, you will see victory. God will help you, but you need to foster good habits. Start today!

Victory

I have life. I have been changed. The transformation process is not complete, but I am not the man I was. I cannot express the difference within me, in my family, and in my relationship with God. Though life is not perfect, and I still face temptations, I know I can walk in purity, and that God can use me to do His will.

I once thought I was beyond help. I once thought I could never be useful in God's hands. I once thought I would wind up dead, or in prison, or suffering from an STD. Instead, I love God and strive to walk in purity. Also, I now have a passion to help others avoid the mistakes I've made. God has truly transformed my life.

How has God used my struggle to do His will? First of all, I have a deep compassion for those who face similar struggles because I know first-hand what it's like to be controlled by something that I know is hurting my family and me. What separates me from the guy in prison or the woman who leaves her husband in hopes of fulfilling her sexual urges? It is only the grace of God. I am no one special. I have simply chosen to receive the help He freely offers. God has delivered me. His word and the Holy Spirit have been my helper and my guide. Apart from God, I truly believe I would be in prison, or suffering through a painful divorce, or infected with a dreadful disease, or perhaps even dead. I know even today, I am just one bad choice away from painful consequences. This reality is sobering.

The second thing God is doing with my past is opening up doors of ministry. God has redeemed my past. He is turning it into a passion to help people avoid my mistakes, and to show people they too can break free from bad habits and addictions. Instead of asking me to hide behind a mask, God has sent me out to share my story, and to give others hope. The Lord not only forgave me and healed me, but He has shown me I am useful to Him. Once I was able to surrender my addiction and submit to His plan for my life, I was able to be a vessel of honor.

Thirdly, God has used my past as a blessing to understand His grace. I know I have sinned greatly, and I know He has forgiven me completely. I cannot express the gratitude within me. I cannot display the joy and thanksgiving that burns in my soul because I know what God has saved me from. The more I am aware of this, the more I am overcome with praise, and the desire to follow Him.

Finally, I am reminded by my thorn in the flesh that I need God. My weakness reminds me of my need of a Savior every day. I must rely on His grace, His strength, His promises, and His Holy Spirit to remain pure. I need God. I cannot fight this battle on my own.

I praise God alone for the transformation that has occurred within me. He has changed my life and rescued me from my private prison cell. He wants to do the same thing for you. Whatever your struggle may be, God is able and willing to help you overcome. It will not be easy. The solution is simple but requires faith and discipline, both of which only you can apply to your life. God will help. God will give you answers. God will open the prison door and lead you out, but you must be willing to follow.

I want to encourage you to take His hand. Let His word be a lamp unto your feet. He will light the way and show you what to do. Then take steps of faith, follow what you know to be true, commit yourself to obey whatever truth God reveals to your heart. If you will trust Him, and make an effort, He will draw closer than you could ever imagine. He will transform your life and bless you incredibly.

There is hope. You can overcome your struggle. You can break free from habitual sin. You can find freedom and enjoy a life after addiction. I am living proof.

Printed in the United States
141373LV00001BA/4/A

9 781604 772982